The
Second-Greatest
BASEBALL GAME
Ever Played

Also by Drew Bridges

Family Lost and Found

Stories from the Sunshine Mountain Valley:
Tales for Reading and Ready for Telling

The
Second-Greatest
BASEBALL GAME
Ever Played

A Memoir

DREW BRIDGES

The Second-Greatest Baseball Game Ever Played

iUniverse books may be ordered through booksellers or by contacting:

iUniverse
1663 Liberty Drive
Bloomington, IN 47403
www.iuniverse.com
1-800-Authors (1-800-288-4677)

ISBN: 978-1-4917-4778-0 (sc)
ISBN: 978-1-4917-4779-7 (hc)
ISBN: 978-1-4917-4777-3 (e)

Library of Congress Control Number: 2014916849

Printed in the United States of America.

iUniverse rev. date: 10/23/2014

CONTENTS

PROLOGUE

THE BROOKLYN DODGERS DEFEATED the New York Yankees in the seventh game of the 1955 World Series in the greatest baseball game ever played. This was the triumph of the underdog, the common man defeating the royalty of the game, the American dream played out on dirt and grass.

Maybe you disagree. Okay, then you pick the greatest baseball game ever played. Maybe it would be Hard-Luck Harvey Haddix's twelve perfect innings that ended in loss, a classic heroic tragedy. Perhaps the greatest game should be any game in 1947 in which Jackie Robinson played, breaking the race barrier. I won't argue. I grant you the right to choose the greatest game.

But for the second-greatest game ever played, I will not yield. The second-greatest baseball game ever played took place on Saturday, June 29, 1957. No Yankees, Giants, Dodgers, Cardinals, or Red Sox were there. No Ruth, Clemente, Ted Williams, or Jackie Robinson went to bat. The game played out in my hometown of Hildebran in western North Carolina. Two teams of boys, ten to fifteen years old, faced off on the high school baseball diamond, no uniforms and no organized league. I played second base, and my brother played third. My dad coached our team.

Why would this game be considered "great"? This game came about because of fate and faith. Fate that my father was one of the lucky ones to come home from World War II along with all those other Americans who returned to the business of getting jobs and raising families. It was fate because at one point my father had already received his orders to go to the Pacific and be a part of the invasion of Japan. Then we dropped the atomic bomb, and he came home.

Fate and faith. Faith because this baseball game represented a promise kept. It was an act of faith by my father and several other men in the Hildebran community a dozen years after their return from war. At that time boys had few organized summer sports activities. Kids were on their own for free time. These men donated their time for what we now call *community building*. Dad and others drove around the rural neighborhoods to find boys who wanted to play sports. He and others spent their own money to buy balls and bats and organize these future young men into a real game. An organized local Little League baseball program ultimately grew from these efforts.

Thousands of other fathers did the same thing for millions of other children, the children known as the baby boomers. But statistics and demographic trends do not tell the story in the way it needs to be told, in detail, with names of ordinary people and descriptions of small communities. I lived this story. Only ten years old in 1957, I remember it as if it were yesterday.

Of course I understood almost nothing of the larger story on that day. It was just a game, albeit a glorious one with a real umpire and guided by the official rule book. I learned more about the context of this game after my father's death in 1997 when I read the letters that he sent to my mother from his service in Italy and a few other places in 1944 and 1945. She saved the letters, ninety-six of them, and I read them all, from greetings to closings. Most are repetitious and show mainly a sad and lonely man wanting to get home to his wife who was pregnant with my brother. But some of the letters are remarkable acts of self-disclosure and reveal to me a man I did not know, despite all of fifty years as his son and what I would call a good relationship.

Charles Steven Bridges, born May 25, 1917, died July 5, 1997, orphaned as a child, became a father and gave back more than he received. He lived, as do we all, an imperfect life. He didn't get everything right, but he got enough of it to send me into the world whole. This is his story, or at least an important part of it, told through the structure of an afternoon of baseball, from my childhood memories and from his letters.

CHAPTER 1

Daddy, Can I Sign Up for
Little League Baseball?

Pfc Charles S. Bridges
ANS34303093
Sgd C-1APO16472-C
C/o Postmaster
New York, NY

Mrs. Charlotte Bridges
PO Box 364
Hildebran, NC

November 11th, 1944

Dear Charlotte,

There is not much use to pop the question "how are you" as it might be a long time before I get any mail from you, however, I am wondering the question over and over in my mind day in and day out, and to keep from going nuts about it I have to brace my mind to the trust that you are O.K. and frame a picture of you and what you are doing. I also frame a picture in my mind of what we will be doing together after the war and I can come home for good, and that picture is what I want to live for. It isn't too bad out here on the ocean when I can live on those thoughts, because those thoughts are strong as it is necessary that I be here and cannot be prevented, and those thoughts make me strong and give me plenty to live for, also with those thoughts I can take advantage of the situation so to speak. I told you in the last letter that we were on the high seas in route to somewhere, well, we are still on the high seas and I don't know how long we will be sailing.

They say the whale was once a land animal. I don't know but I believe I am developing fins. As I said before, the ocean is amazing and interesting, however, for a while I would strain my eyes all over the ocean for something I had not seen, I wanted to see whales, sharks, etc. Anything but a submarine, but all I could see would be water, water, everywhere, but we do have some to drink too, so I just gave it up and take things as a matter of course now, not eager to see amazing new things. I wore myself out looking, after all the ocean is quite a body of water, and to see some things would probably be just a coincidence.

Darling, I trust and hope that you are O.K. and that we are still going to be proud parents, imagine me, imagine you, imagine our little (daughter???) I sing that to the song "Imagine me imagining you" or something like that, maybe you know the exact title, I don't. Anyway Darling, I hope you are O.K. And we are going to have the baby—and I trust that Mother and all the folks are O.K. too and that you have heard good news from Harvey lately—and also that Caesar is alive as ever and I want you to know that I am O.K. After all, the United States Army and Navy is taking care of me and they are pretty strong organization. Also, I love you, adore you, my wonderful adorable wife, and am living for the day I can live with you again.

Love,
Charlie

I WALKED OUT OF my third grade class into a lovely springtime day in 1957. I heard someone call my name. "Hey, Drew! Wait up a minute, will you?"

I turned around to see Ted Icard, Jerry Rudisill, and Louie Page coming toward me fast. I looked around the school yard but saw no sign of my big brother, my only hope to avoid a thrashing at the hands of these older boys. Jerry was in my class, but he had to be at least a year older, because in a few years he and Larry Young would have facial hair long before the rest of us. Ted Icard was the scariest. He had a really dark complexion. I think he had some Lumbee Indian blood, but no one ever talked about anything like that, especially in my house, since he was one of those boys I was supposed to stay away from.

I scanned the road in front of the parking lot to see if my mother had arrived to pick us up from school. No sign of her either. If I cut between two of the yellow school buses lined up for boarding, I would get detention, but that would be better than what those boys likely had in mind for me. I hesitated for only a moment because of the smelly black fumes coming from the tailpipe of the nearest bus, but that was long enough for them to corner me.

"Drew, have you ever thought about signing up for Little League down in Hickory? I think you'd really like it," one of them blurted out.

I trembled so much that I didn't clearly understand the question at first as the three of them formed a menacing arc around me. They couldn't be asking a weakling like me to be a part of their crowd; it must be some kind of joke. I think I sputtered out some kind of answer to them, but at that moment my mother pulled up in our 1950 Ford woody station wagon. I got in the car as quickly as I could. Mother rolled down the window and gave them a look that made them step back.

"Think about it, Drew. We hope you will sign up. It's just a couple of dollars to join," one of them yelled after me.

As I settled into the backseat beside my younger sister, the boys moved closer to the car to take a long look inside. Soon I would understand that they were counting the seats to see how many boys it could carry for the six-mile trip to Hickory, if I could talk my parents into letting me play. That wagon was their only hope to get them to the games.

I knew a good bit about baseball. The Statesville radio station carried the Brooklyn Dodgers games. I'd gone to sleep many nights the previous summer listening to the likes of Duke Snyder, Johnny Podres, and Roy Campanella, but my favorite player was Gil Hodges. More about him later.

I even had a baseball glove. My brother and a few cousins and I played some in our yard, but I never played in a real game on a real field with bases and all that. When I realized that those boys knew a way to be on a team that gave you a uniform and had real umpires, I felt pure joy. My mother already drove to Hickory every Saturday for groceries. I knew six miles was a long way just to play baseball, but I allowed myself to hope. I asked Mother. She said, "Ask your daddy."

Several hours later Dad got out of bed, finally awake from sleeping during the day before his night shift at the Waldensian Sunbeam Bakery in nearby Valdese. When I heard him moving around in the bedroom, I charged into his room and asked if I could help him with his bakery uniform. He wore heavily starched white pants and shirt to work, and someone had to take them off the hanger and loosen them up. My brother and sisters and I often competed for the privilege of running our hands through the shirtsleeves and pant legs to break them open so he could put them on.

I stammered out my question. "So these guys at school told me about how Hildebran boys could sign up for Little League in Hickory … And it only costs a few dollars … And we could all ride together if you or Mom could take us …" And so on.

He wrinkled his face and exhaled. "Aahhh … I just don't see how your mother and I can do it this year. She's got a lot to do for Grandmother now. Maybe next year."

I crumpled inside. I ran out the door and around the back of the house and down into the open dirt basement that slanted down to where we set up nests for our chickens to lay eggs. Two of the hens squawked and beat their wings, throwing dust and feathers into my face as I plopped down on a stack of old drink bottle crates. I cried and whined about how unfair it all was. I picked up small pebbles and dirt clods and threw them at the remains of the old tree stumps that once served as supports for the house before the rough stone columns were added. I vowed to stay down there all night and make them wonder what happened to me. They'd be sorry.

My father changed his mind. I'm not sure why, though I wonder now if it had something to do with another episode of crying and whining, but that time not by me. Dad wanted to move our family to another town, Valdese, and get us out of the old house where we lived with Grandmother. It made sense that he wanted to move the family. Grandmother's house, originally a sawmill shack, bought and enlarged by my grandparents, was old and in need of repairs. It was impossible to heat in the winter with the aging woodstoves, and it had no indoor plumbing beyond one spigot of cold water running from the dug well. So my father had found a house for us in Valdese, not far from the bakery where he worked, with an indoor toilet. I also wonder if he felt a need for some distance from my mother's eight brothers and sisters who lived within walking distance of our house.

I remember clearly my mother's response to his idea to move us. Both she and her mother cried loudly and openly about the possibility. I can see Mother now, on her knees, head to the floor beside the old wringer washer on the back porch, crying and "praying to her God" that somehow the good Lord would change Daddy's mind. Grandmother sat in a chair beside her, rocking back and forth, letting out her emotions in a kind of singsong chant, sobbing. I'm sure Grandmother would have been down there on the floor with Mother if her almost eighty years would have allowed her such mobility.

I don't remember if I cried as I watched all that, but I know I was terrified that I would never see my third-grade girlfriend, Geraldine, again. Even at ten years old I somehow knew that Hildebran girls didn't mix well with Valdese boys. Geraldine didn't actually like me yet, and if we left, all hope would be lost.

As I reflect on my father's change of mind to sign me up for Little League, here is how I understand it. We would stay with my grandmother despite the problems with the old house. Dad would take me and my brother a step out of that small community. He would spend time with us taking us to baseball practices and games. He would make the best of a limited world by making ours a little larger and richer.

CHAPTER 2

Time for a Little Coaching

Sunday, December 19th, 1944

Dear Charlotte,

Today is Sunday and I can picture my wife getting up at about seven o'clock, doing the Sunday morning chores around home, going to church and playing the piano, coming back home, and after noon swarmed in by all kinds of nieces and nephews, then after the evening chores are done she might have gone to another church session, but later, and I hope I am right, I can see her writing a letter to her good for nothing old lazy husband who is somewhere in Italy. Is that about the way things were today, honey? I got another package from you, its contents were all candy. Thanks a million darling, I like the candy you made yourself best of all.

I also got a package from Faye Lou. I think it was the lot of James Wholesale Co. It was sox, cigarettes, stationary, and all kinds of candy. If you see her before she gets the letter of thanks which I am going to write to her, tell her that I thank her very much. I still have not got a letter, but I guess the Christmas season rush is delaying mail these days, so I keep trusting that everything is okay, and one of these days our mail will start hitting us regular. How is Charlotte Jr.? I think Gwendolyn would be a pretty name for her too if you don't agree to Charlotte Laura. Tell Mother hello and give my regards to all.

Good night and sweet dreams.

Love,
Charlie

Summer, 1957

I HEAR IN MY father's December letter a longing for the routine that he would later follow when he returned from the war. My own early memories of life on the small farm had his day begin with the care of the animals and other chores. Then he would sleep through the day before leaving for his night shift at the bakery, a job he held for thirty-plus years. This pattern left some days open for him to drive a station wagon full of boys aged ten to twelve to baseball games in Hickory's Little League.

The Ford woody had three rows of seats, designed for eight passengers. Eventually Dad found a way to crowd four in the back, two on the middle seat, one more on the step leading to the back, and two more boys in the front. That filled out our team of nine. I don't remember seat belts. But on those first trips to Hickory only five or six boys rode with him.

Our team name was "Bots" because the sponsor was the Pepsi-Cola Bottling Company. I wore a big Pepsi-Cola sign on my back.

"That's a pretty dumb name," offered my brother, two years my senior, but I was proud. I had a real uniform.

My brother did not play that first year, something about his birth certificate, but a few of his age-mates did hitch the ride with us. These older boys, Tommy Parham, Tommy Keller, Louie Page, and the others were the baseball gods to me, so strong and skillful. I remember sitting on the top of a dirt bank at one of the older boys' games watching them bang out doubles and triples in a comeback win.

My own debut was less than impressive. Although I had played backyard games with friends and knew the basic structure of the field and some of the rules, I had no idea about where a specific defensive player should position himself in relation to the bases and other players.

My backyard games involved just three or four of us and often had trees or cinder blocks for bases. Boundaries were approximate or nonexistent.

After a few team practice sessions on a converted football field, I finally got to see the field on which we were to play a real game. I remember thinking it was magnificent. Perfectly square bases were tied in place to metal spikes underneath, and there was an elevated pitcher's mound. The dirt infield was flat and rock-free, the outfield grass was mowed like a rich man's front lawn, and the unbelievably straight chalk foul lines extended unbroken from home plate to the outfield fence. Blue sky and bright sun high in the sky completed the spectacle.

"Bridges," the Bots coach yelled, "second base! You're on second base now." It was somewhere around the third inning, and I cheerfully trotted out and stood on top of second base.

"Bridges! Over to your left! Move to the left. Get off the bag," shouted the coach and a number of the other players. All the shouting and waving of arms to reposition me only added to my confusion. Eventually I found the correct spot between first and second, in perfect position to have two ground balls roll through my legs for errors.

My time at bat was more of the same. I couldn't believe how hard and fast that ball was coming toward me. The batting helmet made my head feel heavy and hot. When the second strike flew by me, I remember thinking, *He's got me now.* I swung hard at the next pitch but missed completely. As I walked back to the bench, I took some pride in the coach's words: "Good cut, Bridges, good try."

At that time of my life I was a generally even-tempered lad, and despite my struggles on the field I ended the game in a cheerful mood. I had fun! I played in a real game! My dad, on the other hand, was more impressed with the work that needed to be done.

"I think we need to stay around just a little and let me give you a few tips," he insisted as the other participants cleared the field. We spent the next hour or so reviewing the basics of playing second base. I still remember this first coaching lesson but not so much for the content. I have from that day my most enduring early memory of him as he moved around the baseball diamond, still dressed in his bakery whites from the night before, showing me the proper defensive stances and placement on the field and how to hold my arms and move my feet when going for the ball. His face held the tough, square-jawed determination that shows in his soldier portrait. He was teaching me a game, but this was important to him, and it became important to me.

Where was my mother in all this? She was supportive, more than simply accepting, and did her share of driving us around, but her heart and energies were elsewhere. The story that came down through the family cast Mother as the child who could not leave home as long as the old folks were still alive. She was the youngest of the ten children who survived to adulthood, so she became my grandmother's caretaker. Mother gained permission to marry my father only because he already had his orders to go to war, and my grandparents figured he wouldn't be coming home but his pension would. The story is probably mythology, because who can know the hearts and minds of those long gone, but it's the story that is told.

I also confess I know my mother's heart less than my father's, partly because her letters to him did not survive. By the time I generated a mature curiosity about those years of her life, she had died. What I do believe about my mother is that if she had her way, she would have held me too close and protected me too much. She would never have allowed me to step into the batter's box to face a hard-throwing left-hander. She lived the entire sixty-nine years of her life on the same few acres of land. She lived lovingly and successfully but also perhaps as narrowly as one can live. So this story is not her story. And if she had learned what happened once in Hickory after a game, she would have jerked me out of that crowd immediately. The incident occurred when I and a handful of boys were playing on a swing set as we waited for our ride home.

I had the seat in the big swing first. The older boys came later, but I was there first, just swinging back and forth on a warm Saturday afternoon in June. The smell of freshly cut grass and the blue, blue sky completed my peaceful place in the world. I slipped out of the swing for just a moment to tie my shoe, and Ted Icard jumped in the swing behind me. Not fair. I was taught to wait my turn, and he didn't. He just pushed his way in when I wasn't looking.

"Hey! That was my swing," I protested. He kicked his feet, pumped hard, and began to climb higher and higher. But it was my swing. This shouldn't happen, but he was older, bigger. What could I do?

Several boys yelled to me, "So if you want him out of the swing, make him!"

"Make him! Make him get out of the swing!" others joined the chorus, adding to my embarrassment. I couldn't make Ted Icard do anything. I was humiliated. As I slumped away, I tried to save a bit of my dignity by saying something to him that I'd heard some of my older cousins say. I thought it would be a good comeback. I thought it was clever. If I couldn't make him give me my swing back, at least I would give him a good swipe with words.

"I don't make niggers in my factory."

He leaped out of that swing without slowing down and rushed toward me, his fist clenched, his face in my face before I closed my mouth from the last of my words. He didn't actually hit me, but the force of his presence made me fall back. He stood straddled above me, face reddened, eyes bulging, spittle spraying from his lips.

"What did you call me? Say it again! Say it just one more time!"

Just like my stint on second base, this was not my finest hour. Not only did I cower and tremble sufficiently for him to spare me, but after he let me up, just before our ride got there, I actually went back to him and asked him to please not tell my mother what had happened. Of course neither he nor any of the other boys were about to say anything. They weren't about to mess up the free ride in the woody.

Such was my character in 1957. The words *wimpy* and *clueless* would be accurate. My later life success—paying for college with athletic scholarships and enduring the rigors of medical school and thirty-plus years of taking care of very sick patients—seemed unlikely at the time. Any resilience or toughness I ultimately found came from my sports coaches, and my father was the first. Even then I had a sense that not all boys had fathers involved in their lives, but only later would I understand how important that would be.

Today I sometimes try to call up images of him from when I was very young. From the back porch of the old house, standing beside the wringer washer, one could see the old dug-well cover with bucket and hand crank, the outhouse, the thirty-by-fifty-foot barn with hayloft, and the one-acre garden and corncrib. I wish I could remember more about what he actually looked like as he went about the morning farmwork, but the best I can do is picture a recreated image from some old photos, fuzzy memories, and my imagination.

The chores included carrying a pair of big buckets filled with slop for the pig, and I do remember him squatting beside the cow, his hands working strong streams of milk into a pail. I did only a little of that as I got older, as time gave way for modern things. By 1957 we even had our first television. It had two channels. One carried a baseball game every Saturday. But I was doing more than watching now. I was on a team and in the game.

CHAPTER 3

The Local Team

April 24th, 1945

Dear Charlotte,

Do you know what I done went and done, girlie? I done went and got two letters from you today and one yesterday, but that is not too many, I could stand another one tomorrow and the next day and the next day and the next and on and on—how far I don't know how long, we'll say indefinitely, I'm glad you are okay—much, much glad. It makes me feel good to know you are okay.

Yes, I'll be down on Sunday night some more times, too, but you aren't chasing me home at eleven any more, don't forget that either. When coughing starts in the other room and you start telling me I have to go that you have to go to bed, I'll just tell you to go chase yourself by granny.

Gee there will be quite some difference in our brat and its cousin Faye Lou. I'll bet our brat will call her Aunt Faye. Did Marjorie make a picture of you too to send me, that's what I want and if she didn't, make her take one.

Honey, ask Dr. Palmer if its best to have the baby circumcised, and if he says it is then have it done. I don't know why they do, but everybody has it done these days.

Your know honey, that's a funny thing, you for some reason like to get letters from me, and I never realized it so much before, but now I for some reason like to write letters to you. As for getting them from you, that's a dose of a medicine that I am doped with and couldn't survive without getting them. When I get them late I get all nervous and torn up, and just have to have them that's all there is to it. Gone too far to stop now.

Would you cut my toenails if I were in that predicament? Would you??? When I last saw my wife she was not that big all over, she was just a nice big arm full of lovely female wife. Blame me! Blame me! Gee whiz woman there is oceans and continents between you and me, and you blame me for getting kicked in the belly. Say who am I? Anyway? I'll bet baby is going to be a mean tough critter, you teach him to be good and I'll teach him to be mean and he should have a pretty good mixture of natural tact.

Honey I don't really need all those things I ask you to send me, except the hair oil. I'll need the stationery too, when this gives out.

Yes I guess I am your old man, and I will be your boss too, when I get back home. Well, maybe I can't lose your love like a packet comb, but I will keep looking to see if I have lost it anyway. Where are you going so much, that you are in your way? Listen here you to me now, you slow down to a most comfortable speed and stay that way yes, stay that way, your hurrying so much, and working so much days are finished, you yourself count more than what you accomplished by working like the devil. Capito?

Well, honey I will settle for a boy if he is a boy, we won't trade him to anyone for a girl. The next one will be a sweet tootsie like her mom. You are "it" honey, but not because merely that you are loved by me, although I wouldn't love you if you weren't.

I wish I could send my mother-in-law something for a mother's day gift, but I don't think I will be able to. I will be thinking of my baby's mother most of all. She is my baby's mother and my wife. One more week in this month honey, and then the long stretch begins. I hardly think Ralph could cross an ocean to be with Ethel if she were having baby if he were controlled by the same circumstances I am, because if it were possible I would be right there in body with you when the baby is born, but so far it is impossible. It would take a miracle to get me there in body, but I will be there in heart, soul and mind, you can depend on that.

Love,
Charlie

Lazy summer days

DESPITE HIS LACK OF formal education, most of my father's letters show a coherence of thought and theme. His April 24 letter, however, is notable for a rambling and I think anxious quality. With the birth of his first child a month away and him in Italy, I hear him struggling to find words to ask whether a family will really be there when he returns. It helps to understand him to know he spent a number of years in an orphanage. His own childhood experiences, from what I know, could not have presented him with a model of how to be a part of a family. His letter seems to alternate between a controlling voice and a needy one.

Like so many World War II veterans, he revealed little of his actual overseas experiences. Many letters were clearly censored, and some pages had dates and locations neatly cut out of the paper. Back home he always showed a reluctance to tell war stories, even in later years. Perhaps I was too cautious with questions. I think he was spared the experience of direct combat, but he did speak of the hardships of labor and one time spoke briefly of "the most miserable night on a beach that you could imagine." Despite all this, the uncertainty and the hardships, by the time I was a ten-year-old second baseman, he had found a way to be the boss, the husband, and now the coach.

The regular season in Hickory Little League ended early in the summer to allow time for the selection of the all-star team and the statewide competition. Since I, obviously, did not make the all-stars, a lot of summer remained after my season ended. I was not ready to give this up, and more importantly, neither was my father. Before long we were riding around Hildebran in the woody station wagon, looking for boys the same age of me and my brother who wanted to play more ball. I remember sitting in the wagon while Dad met with the local high school principal and sports coaches to get permission to use the Hildebran High School baseball field. Only much later did I have any idea about the work he did to convince the local powers to go along with his plans.

⸛

Some of that summer I spent playing with my younger cousin Winston. I liked the fact that I was older and could usually best him, although our skills were comparable. Many days his father, Horace, would drop him off at my house, and we would walk the mile to the ball field. First we would go past or cut through Cline Cemetery, where my older cousins took me one night to show me a mysterious light, of course to sneak away and leave me there alone as others made spooky sounds from behind tombstones.

Our path would then take us down into the huge red dirt gash in the landscape where the unfinished Interstate Highway 40 snaked through the neighborhood. That winter, before the highway opened to traffic, scores of local kids used cardboard sleds for some great sledding down the long, frozen, snow-covered embankments. In better weather the six-foot-diameter drainage culverts made for great hide-and-seek. One Sunday afternoon my brother found a way to crank up one of the unattended giant earthmoving machines and did some impressive damage to some pine trees.

Drawing closer to the center of the town, Winston and I often paused to look up at the highest hill in the neighborhood to admire the Aderholt house. The impressive show of giant round columns marked it clearly as the most grand of homes in the area, built with the wealth of the local textile mills. Anyone with money in Hildebran got it from furniture or socks. Moving on, we sometimes had enough change in our pockets to stop for a six-cent Pepsi-Cola from Freuller's Grocery. I remember the day I went into the store with only a nickel and found they had attached an extra piece of equipment on the machine, a small box into which you had to put another penny to get the drink. I couldn't believe that a nickel would no longer buy you a Pepsi.

The store's owner and namesake spoke with a heavy German accent.

It was common knowledge that during the war the government sent some people down from Washington to keep an eye on him to make sure he was not passing secrets to the enemy.

What a sight the two of us must have been. A ten-year-old and an eight-year-old carrying beat-up baseball gloves and a dirty worn ball; dragging a bat behind us; decked out in shorts, T-shirts, and street shoes; sporting our flattop haircuts grown too long to stand up; sipping on our Pepsi-Colas.

Finally at the ball field, we usually found it deserted. Any chalk lines from the school-year games were long since erased by wind and rain, no real bases left out. The once-manicured grass was overgrown in places, invaded by weeds and large stands of clover. But there was a metal backstop, so when we pitched to each other and missed the ball, it would bounce back promptly. Only when one of us managed to actually hit the ball did we have to run to retrieve it.

The overall shape of the field was unusual, laid out as a narrow rectangle with left field much longer than any ordinary field. The ball would roll forever if it got past the left fielder. The short right field ended with a sharp drop-off down an embankment that led to the open sewer for the school. Hitting the ball over the right-field bank usually meant you lost it to the sewer, but there was also a sandpit settling and drying area where lost balls sometimes showed up. Winston and I retrieved several balls from that inglorious oblivion. No matter what had soaked into these balls, a little time in the sun and they were fine, although they still felt a little heavy.

These hot, lazy hours filled our afternoons, leaving us sunburned but never in any kind of danger. Everyone who saw us knew who we were and who our parents were. Had we tried any sort of mischief, either Aunt Irene or my mother would know about it before we got home. If the telephone party line was busy, a lot of people would know about it.

Once we almost got ourselves in trouble, in another little store a half mile down the road toward Henry River Mill Village. I believe the man who ran the store was named Cline, and he was blind. Legend held that if you gave him a paper money bill he could tell whether it was a one-, five-, ten-, or twenty-dollar bill. We decided to test him.

I chose a Baby Ruth candy bar, and Winston picked up some Sugar Babies. We handed him a one-dollar bill and told him it was a twenty. He took it and held it in his hands, rubbing the paper between his thumb and index finger. He took a deep breath and ran his finger along the edge and paused for just a second. We knew we were found out ten seconds after he took the bill. I saw the telephone on the wall beside him, and I knew that Mother was at home. Sweat popped out on my forehead; I looked at Winston, and he was as red as a sunburn.

Mr. Cline rocked back in his chair and turned his face to the ceiling, eyes closed behind his dark glasses, still holding the bill with two hands, the heels of his palms touching the counter for balance. He shrugged, and one of the suspenders of his coveralls fell down over the arm of his red checkered shirt. He rocked back forward and reached to rearrange his clothes and in one motion handed the bill back to me.

"You know, boys ..." He spoke the words as if they were a question, hesitated briefly, then continued, "I don't rightly think I have enough change in my register to break a twenty today, so I'm gonna just let you have those things for free today. It's on me. And you come back anytime when you have some money that's not in such a big bill."

I think we were able to leave the store without running. I did take my dollar back, and we kept the candy. Once outside we took off running and didn't stop until we reached the shelter of a big oak tree not far from my house. We sat down and looked at each other but didn't talk. Two people who had just escaped a hanging didn't really need to talk to communicate. I didn't eat the Baby Ruth until the next day.

⚬

Winston was too young to be a part of the real games. At age ten I was one of the youngest and usually rode in the front seat of the wagon as an often noisy group of older boys filled out the back of the woody. For several weeks leading up the second-greatest game, Dad took us all for practices on the Hildebran High School ball field. At one point, to prepare the field, he tied a large wooden plat to a rope behind the station wagon and dragged it across the infield. There was no shortage of boys who volunteered to ride on the device to give it extra weight, so it could do a better job scraping and smoothing the field. Apparently no mothers of any of the boys heard about this part, so no complaints were ever registered.

My brother first practiced in left field but then moved to third base. At age eleven he could catch a ball in the air or on the ground as well as anyone his age. Tommy Keller, one of the best athletes on the team, alternated between center field and shortstop. I was installed in my glory position at second base. Jerry Rudisill and Louie Page tried out several positions, Jerry settling on first base.

All these boys had real skill in throwing, catching, and hitting, but most of their experience was in backyards and open fields, sometimes with fence posts or car fenders subbing as bases. In these four or five practices, Dad worked hard to clarify the actual rules of the game and the finer points of playing their positions. They were eager to learn. According to my mother, some of them came from less than "respectable" families, but they showed nothing but respect for my father and what he was trying to accomplish.

For my part, I continued my pattern of embarrassing my father. One day as we were taking the crew of older boys home, with me riding in the front seat, we passed a large pigpen in the side yard of a farmhouse. I called out to the others in a loud clear voice, "Hey, look there, everybody; one of those pigs is riding on the back of the other one!" One might have thought that growing up on a small farm I would have known what I was looking at, but at that point I was still the young, clueless one in the car. Dad just kept looking forward where he was going. The snickers from the backseat soon died out.

CHAPTER 4

Let's Play Ball

May 11th, 1945

Dear Charlotte,

Hey there—I got back to my outfit today and found some more letters from my sweet old wife. That's just swell too. I like letters from my wifey. The last one written that I have received was written May 2. And I got the one with the pictures of our little boy's clothes. Gee that is a swell bunch of clothes. The picture made me feel good and made me think more about my little old tot, in a way that I was closer to him, and my wife, in a way that I am proud of her and I love her more. Gee honey, I am sorry that you didn't get all those things that I never sent you, maybe you will get them sometime, because I did want to send them. I got a letter from Edgar too, he seems to be giving his post war plans pretty deep consideration. He can get the bill of rights benefit of going to college, but his worry is if he can stick to his studies and make it really worth his while. So you think you rate in my life do you. Well you aren't the only one who rates in my life by granny, that little old baby rates in my life too. Okay! Okay! You can have all the red headed things, but there aren't going to be any. All of 'em have to be mine, and they ain't going to be red headed, see! Of all the things, you are really going to blame me for your being kicked in the belly, and as far as I am from you too. Well, lots of people say a guy must play the devil when he gets married, that his wife will just blame everything on him, everything! Even if he is innocent. Well, I was warned, so I guess I have to take the consequences. Didn't you tell him what I said about kicking his mother. If you let him get away without obeying his first order, gee, he will be hard for me to handle and then I'll blame you.

Yeah! You just try cutting down on your writing, just try, but you had better not succeed by granny. I want three letters each day. One for breakfast, one for dinner and one for supper. And gosh honey, after June the fifth those letters can double up, one from my little daughter with every one from my wife. Due to her age though, I won't raise too much cane if I don't get three a day from her. Gee gosh, I'm looking forward to lots of mail from my wife and daughter together. You will make her write to me won't you honey? I will cut your toenails honey if you will make her write to me, and if you won't cut down on your writing. A bargain???

Well honey, I guess I could tell you more about what I do. When I first came over I was in a place pretty close to the real McCoy. I never was in actual combat, but the living conditions were rough as all get out, and Jerry came over a few times, but most of the time he must have been just taking pictures, then it seemed things just changed overnight. I guess the fighting moved further away, and they knew they had things pretty well under control and would not have to use some of us in actual combat, then I was transferred to this outfit. I have been used on the ground for different things. This outfit done plenty in the war, they wear about seven battle stars, and a presidential citation badge. Of course the ground crew was back at the base when the flying personnel was in action. Some times we left the base to go to another airfield closer to the mission objective to prepare them for the mission. That's as far as I ever got. Anyway, I don't know what the ground crew went through in Africa and Sicily.

Lately we have been able to see movies, they show them with the small 16 mm projector, and they have regular movies in Naples. I have had no time for playing any kind of ball since I have been over here. As far as the Italian girls, honey, there is no kind of female anywhere that can make me forget about you, not even for one minute. I'm done sold *on the idea that you are it. You are my wife and you are the mother of my brat. You see I sorta like my wife and I am set on her for life. If Marjorie could have taken that picture of baby's clothes she could have got you in with them. And my baby too. Aren't I going to get any pictures of you taken in the Month of May? I want a picture of you and baby for a birthday present. I want my baby regardless of what day she is born – the day will be a distinguished one for the fact she was born then. I want my wife right now and always. I've got her too, that's some what of a consolation even though we are deprived of the close companionship and ecstasy at the present time. I've got you to come home too, and not only you, I've got a tot and you to come home too.*

Are you suffering very much now honey? I am with you darling, and I am hoping and praying that you will be okay.

Love
Your husband

I SUPPOSE IT IS not surprising that the sweetness and playful banter in my father's letters to my mother might not represent the way the rest of the world saw him in later years. By the time Dad pulled up with a station wagon full of ten- to twelve-year-old boys for the first organized baseball game in Hildebran, a different atmosphere prevailed at home. He now had five "tots" or "brats" as he previously described his firstborn. As in all families, joys came alongside hardship. On the day of that game I sat in the middle of the front seat. My brother, who was the object of my father's original fatherhood dreams and fantasies, sat to my right. Seven neighborhood boys who we had picked up from various places around the community filled up the two backseats.

As soon as we got out of the woody, Dad saw the problem. He had worked a verbal agreement with Paul Fowler, an older boy from town who was known for his zeal for the game, to organize the other team. Dad thought he had been clear about the ages of the players he would bring, and he expected Paul to bring the same. Whether Paul misunderstood or simply brought his buddies was not clear. But it was very clear that we were lined up against boys one to three years older than our oldest player. The difference between ten- to twelve-year-olds and those aged thirteen or fourteen is huge in terms of baseball skills.

There might have been some discussion about mixing up the teams to balance things out—I don't know what transpired between Dad and Paul—but as our team started to warm up our throwing arms and go through the standard pregame rituals, I saw an angry and determined look come over Dad. I then watched him jump back in the vehicle and speed away. A half hour later he was back with two more boys.

Paul walked over to the three of them and said, "Wait a dern minute now: you can't play those guys. They're way too big for—"

Dad came back quickly, "Okay, I got my pencil in my hand, and I got a clipboard. I know almost all the players on your team and how old they are. Let's add up the ages and divide by nine." Dad took a ten-dollar bill out of his wallet and put it on the ground directly in front of Paul. "If your number's lower than mine, you keep the money, and I won't play 'em." He continued to stare Paul down with a look that was intimidating, perhaps overly so between an adult and a teenager. Paul looked back at his team, then looked around at ours, then silently turned and walked away, defeated. The game was on.

The first of our two new players was Billy Cline, not really older than Paul or some of his team, but even at fourteen years old, he was a striking figure of an athlete. He would later set football offensive records for East Carolina University that still stand today. He then played for the Ottawa Roughriders in the Grey Cup in the Canadian Football League. His brother, Doug, anchored the line for the Houston Oilers for the American Football League. Today they raise thoroughbred horses in Georgia.

The second player was Druey Lambert, to my memory an even more imposing figure of a man-boy. Some of that may have been because he was the only boy I ever met who had a missing finger. This did not get in the way of his baseball skills, though. I think he lost it working in a sawmill. I don't believe they had OSHA back then.

Billy pitched, and Druey was the catcher. While they were roughly the same age as some of Paul's guys, even in warm-up one could see they possessed a higher level of skill. They lived in Valdese, ten miles west, where Dad had spent his later high school years. He maintained connections there and knew the local athletes. Valdese was a bigger community with a larger high school. Boys in the larger town had more opportunities for learning the games and developing their skills. Dad wanted to bring such opportunities to Hildebran, since he couldn't take me and my brother to Valdese.

Valdese once had a college called Rutherford College that had a football team when Dad was in high school, in the 1930s. Dad often told the story that after playing for Valdese High on Friday night, he would dress out with the college team on Saturday night. He played center, lining up next to Clarence Stasavich, who became a legendary small-college coach at Lenoir-Rhyne College, winning an NAIA National Championship in 1960. Stasavich then moved to East Carolina University, then known as East Carolina Teachers College, where he coached Billy Cline to a win in the Tangerine Bowl in 1964.

Whether any of Paul's boys knew Billy or Druey, and whether or not they knew what they were up against, I don't know, but they settled into the game with quiet, serious looks on their faces. As someone who was still early in learning the rules of this game, I remember how disciplined and well informed all the others were about how a game should proceed. Baseball has formal rules, but it also has traditions and rituals beyond what is written anywhere. There are the ways that infielders warm up before an inning and where and how batters stand when they are next up to bat. Knowing these things separates the novices from those who really know baseball.

A few other things stand out in my memory. All these boys were nothing but respectful to each other and to the adults around once the game started. No one cursed, not once. No one trash-talked, not once. In those days, in that community, it was not uncommon for a parent to take a bar of soap to the mouth of a child should certain words come out.

Another thing that I think fits with their respectfulness and their seriousness was that every boy that showed up that day had a baseball glove. All these boys were from families of modest means. Some even "went to bed hungry"—according to my mother, who would say this while reminding me and my siblings that we never missed a meal—but everyone had a baseball glove. Like a Bible and a rifle, it was just one of those things that your family had.

I think a lot of my father's love of sports was about the rules. Although I know too little about his childhood, I know enough to know it was not a fair game. His mother died when he was eight years old, and his father died when he was ten.

He once told me the story of his mother's death. She was bedridden, and he was attending her when she died. Apparently her death was not expected to be imminent, because he remembers a lot of anger and yelling when his father came in the room and found that she had passed. My father felt responsible but not sure what he had done wrong.

Following his father's death, my father and his two brothers and three sisters lived briefly with relatives then went to an orphanage, the Mills Home in Thomasville, North Carolina. While many stories about orphanages are horror stories, my father recalled his several years there in a very positive way. He describes a sense of "order" and a comforting set of expectations about daily life, although he never said it in quite those words. I think a sense of order was absent from his life before the Mills Home. At the orphanage there were rules. When he was there, the orphans worked for their supper. He said this not as a complaint but as useful learning and with a sense of pride. He rose early every day, milked cows, collected eggs from the chickens, and learned about running a farm by doing it.

Then there were the games. His favorite was an informal one called "bringin' in," a freeform version of football. The rules were simple. The action began with a boy with a football in the middle of a single straight line, boys spread out on both sides. The one with the ball would kick it as far as he could, and all would chase it with an every-man-for-himself dash. The boy with the speed to retrieve the prize was then on his own to "bring it in" to the original starting place.

Dad never actually said it, but the way he told the story of this game suggested he was the bringin'-in champion among his peers. His speech and body language transformed during the telling, head held high, shoulders back, jaw set and determined.

There was another game that was more problematic. A railroad track ran next to the campus, and the train would slow as it moved through the area. The object of this game was to jump aboard the train and hold onto the ladders on the sides of the freight cars as it left, gathering speed. The last one to jump off won the game. While never a sanctioned activity by the leaders of the orphanage, the game was effectively outlawed when a boy lost an arm under the train's wheels.

Dad never admitted playing this game, and his manner of telling it indicated clearly this was a cautionary tale for a young boy.

Years later, I once asked Dad if children were ever abused or mistreated by the adults at the orphanage, referencing a newspaper report about a modern-day scandal in another state. He answered quickly and with confidence that his caretakers were never anything but kind and caring people.

Back to the letters. I personally don't remember the sweet, sentimental side of my father. I don't know where it came from or where it went. I did see and gained immeasurably from his love of games and the rules. I think I adopted some of his attitude, that certain look he could muster, like when he stared down Paul or when he talked about bringin' in. He had that look when he scanned the infield and saw Billy pitching and Druey catching. The look said it all. Shoulders back, standing tall, jaw strong and set. Focused.

"We can take these guys."

CHAPTER 5

Batter Up!

June 5th, 1945

Dear Charlotte,

Darling, I got a letter from you today written May 30, my baby is born and you are okay. That's wonderful! And I am happy. What kind of little old boy do we have honey? Does he cry much—does he look like his mother? I like his mother, I wish I could see my wife and baby. I'll bet he will favor his Uncle Ralph and Uncle Edgar. Who does he favor now? He is like his daddy in the way he likes to sleep, by granny. Yes darling he was a wonderful birthday present. What we going to do with him darling: You know what I could bring him if I were coming home from here—I could bring him a little monkey. There is beaucoup of them in the jungles on this island. And I'll bet he would be the envy of all the kids in the neighborhood if he had a little live monkey for a pet. I wish I were coming home now. I would bring him one.

I got a letter from Ethel today—she said everybody was okay.

Does my boy ever smile honey? Does he cry? Did someone send announcements to the relatives? Has any of them come to see you since he was born? What does Lucy have to say about him? You know what I would like to do—I would like come see you and my tot, by granny—and I would like to stay with you and my tot when I get there too. Tell him I said Goochy! Goochy! And be good to his mother. I haven't written to anyone but you since I left Italy—I've been sorta busy—you can tell the relatives where I am if they come see you. I don't know how long I will be here in Trinidad—and I don't know where I will go when I leave here. I wish I were going home to my family. And I wish it were soon if not sooner. I love my family. I don't have time to write more now but I'm all excited about my family and I am happy that he is born and that you are okay. Give my love to my wife and baby darling.

Love, Charlie

MY FATHER'S FIRST LETTER about his newborn son came exactly four weeks after the war ended in Europe. Hitler's surrender allowed him and many other soldiers to leave Italy. What the letter does not say is that when he was in Trinidad, he learned he was being reassigned to the Pacific Theater and would be a part of the invasion of Japan. If he knew his assignment when he wrote on June 5, nothing in his letter betrayed his worry. His thoughts were all about family and his future. But in August everything would change. Two atomic bombs fell on Japan and speeded his return home.

"Batter up!" cried the man who had volunteered to umpire this game, the first of its kind for boys this age in Hildebran. His name was Melvin Ruggles, a native Pennsylvanian who came to the high school to teach and coach basketball. He was one of the few Yankees in the school and the town. In 1964 he coached Hildebran High School's boys' basketball team to a state championship and a perfect 29–0 record. As one of the first subs on that team, I remember our team entered the gym in Winston Salem for the finals sporting matching blue blazers Ruggles had arranged for us. I never knew exactly who donated the money for the blazers. Some members of that team came from families that could not have afforded that small piece of elegance. It was the most expensive item of clothing I owned up to that point in time.

But on this warm day in June 1957, no one had anything close to a uniform. Blue jeans, sweatpants, gym shorts, and T-shirts were the dress of the day. I doubt anyone had shoes with spikes. Instead we had canvas tennis or basketball shoes or regular street shoes.

A coin flip put Paul's boys up to bat first. I ran out to my position at second base; at least I knew where to stand this time. Jerry Rudisill, one of the boys who had me ask my parents to let me play in Hickory, took his position to my left at first base. Tommy Keller, an age-mate of my brother, held down shortstop, and my brother, Mills, played third base.

The real athletes on our side, the real skill players, were Billy Cline pitching and Druey Lambert behind the plate. As Billy finished the last of his warm-up throws, the rest of us in the field began our chatter, so much an integral part of the game.

"Hey, batter, batter ..."

"Fire it in there, Billy, Billy, Billy ..."

"Come, Babe, hum, Babe, you the one, you the one ..."

Their first man stood in to bat, Roger Smith, their shortstop. I think he was fourteen years old at the time, a good athlete who later played high school baseball. He took two quick strikes and then caught a piece of a curveball and rolled it slowly toward shortstop. Tommy had trouble getting it out of his glove, and Roger beat the throw to first. They had their leadoff man on base. Billy retrieved the ball and pounded it into his glove, showing a bit of frustration. The first batter should have been an out.

Batting second was Jessie "Punk" Raby, easily the biggest boy on the field, wide and tall, and later a star tackle for the high school football team. I don't know about the nickname. I doubt it had to do with his character, maybe his shape.

After Billy threw the next pitch, high and wide for a ball, Dad called a time-out and went to the mound to talk to Billy. I think he wanted to make sure the game wasn't getting away from us at the start. Dad noticed that the chatter had died down. All the noise, all the enthusiasm, was on the other side. He said only one word to Billy, a word I did not hear. Then he turned his back to Billy and shouted to the rest of us, "Let's go! What happened to the chatter? Stand up here! Let's play or go home!"

"Hey, batter, batter ..."

"You the one, Billy, Billy ..."

"Fire it in there ... Here we go ... Yeah, boy, yeah, boy ..."

Billy responded. He threw three hard fastballs, each just a little higher and harder than the one before it. Jessie took three hard swings and then made the slow walk back to the bench.

Up next was Herb Livertt. He looked like an athlete—strong, lean, tall. Later he did some fighting on the Golden Gloves boxing circuit. He stepped into the batter's box confidently, determined, and took three pitches without offering to swing, studying, waiting, sizing up his foe. Two balls, one strike. Then after two foul balls, one of which he barely got a nick of it to keep his bat alive, he looked as if he were on the defensive, set up for a strikeout. He looked awkward and uncertain now at the plate. But the next pitch came too far inside and clipped his shirt. Hit batsman. Ruggles signaled him to take first base.

A few of our boys offered a meek protest, more of a whine, saying that Herb did not try to get out of the way and should not have been awarded first base. Ruggles was having none of that. "Play ball! Next batter up!"

Two men on base. Only one out. And Paul Fowler was coming to the plate.

At this point in his life, Paul was known by his friends as a kind of Mr. Baseball. I once heard that in February or March he would unplug all the televisions in his house and not turn them back on until baseball season was over. He believed that television was bad for his eyes, and he would let nothing get in the way of hitting a baseball. In the summer he would turn his radio to KDKA for Pittsburg Pirate baseball or the Statesville station that carried the Brooklyn Dodgers.

But usually as long as there was daylight, Paul would work on his game. Most boys his age, in those days, did not do a lot of "training," other than just playing a lot. Paul was the exception. He had a series of workouts he would go through—running bases, throwing, and more— to develop his game. I got all this information from my cousin Winston, who said he watched Paul go through his paces day after day.

Paul also had a series of rituals that he performed when he was batting. Some modern baseball players do this today, a series of choreographed habits or motions, all in the same order to get set to hit. But Paul was the first person back then whom I saw do this. He would step into the batter's box left foot first, straighten his belt buckle with his left hand, then reach around to the back of his belt and pull his trousers up with a quick jerk. He would tap the plate three times with the bat, bend over low at the waist, straighten back up, bend the knees, cock his bat, and then look up quickly at the pitcher as if he was startled, and he was then ready for action.

Billy came with the first pitch to him hard and fast but right down the middle of the plate, in Paul's power zone. Paul swung hard with a loud grunt and connected. The ball leaped off the bat and soared high into left field. It passed over the head of our left fielder and continued to rise.

As I mentioned before, this baseball field had an odd shape, more like a rectangular football field than the usual symmetrical pattern, with a very long left field and a short right field. Where left field ended stood a two-story wood-frame house bordering the school property. The ball traveled a long way to get to the house. Years later I measured the distance from home plate to the base of the house at 454 feet. The ball hit the side of the house just below an upstairs window.

I think it would be fair to say the ball would have traveled easily five hundred feet. Major league power-hitting legends, such as Mickey Mantle and Frank Howard were known to hit balls that far, but Paul Fowler was a midteenager.

"Foul ball!" yelled Ruggles.

"What!" the other team cried out in unison.

"That ball went right over the left fielder's head!" someone shouted. The entire team rushed to the plate to raise their protest.

Ruggles took off his umpire's mask, wiped his ruffled hair back into place and returned his baseball cap to his head. He motioned for Dad and Paul to come to the side of the backstop where he would explain his ruling, as soon as the other players on the team returned to the bench.

Order then restored, Ruggles explained, "When we set the ground rules, we did not say anything about where the left field foul line ends. And since there is no fence for the ball to go over, we have to put the end of the foul line at the house. Yes, the ball was fair most of the way, but it went so far that when it hit the house, it was in foul territory."

Ruggles looked at Paul for a reaction. None came. He looked at Dad for comment. No reply. Ruggles turned away slowly, walked over to the plate, brushed it clear of dirt, and took his position. He straightened his protective mask and barked, "Foul ball! Batter up!"

What Melvin Ruggles explained is that most baseball fields have boundaries clearly delineated with a fence, and where the ball passes over the fence is the point at which it is judged fair or foul. The absence of a fence or another specified end to the playing field led to his decision that the house would serve as the boundary.

Paul stepped back in. He straightened his belt buckle, jerked his trousers, tapped the plate three times, bent at the waist, back up, bent his knees, cocked his bat, and glared at the pitcher. Billy called time-out and called Druey to the mound. Lots of nodding between them. Both spit on the ground in unison. Meeting over, the opponents faced off.

A long, slow, sweeping curveball arched toward the plate. Paul was out in front of the pitch, swung and missed, and tumbled to the ground over to the other side of the batter's box. He bounced up quickly and dusted himself off. He stepped back in, left foot first, belt buckle, jerk pants, tap three times, bend, straighten, bend knees, cock the bat, glare.

Billy threw another curveball. Paul let it go by for a ball. Billy's fastball came inside, ball two. Another fastball drifted far outside. The count was now full. Three balls, two strikes. Runners on first and second base. One out. Billy stepped off the back of the pitcher's mound and took a deep breath. He readied himself, rejected the first sign that Druey put down, then nodded his head, and delivered.

Another curveball came looping toward the strike zone. Paul's sharp eye saw it would be a strike. He anticipated that it would be a slow curve. He waited. Waited. He was ready. He swung viciously and hit the ball solidly in the sweet spot of the bat. The ball screeched toward me ... at my head! I put up my glove in front of my face in self-defense.

Smaaaacccckkkk! The ball lodged tightly in my glove. I opened my eyes to see the runner from first base desperately trying to stop and go back. He practically ran over me. I reached out my glove and tagged him.

Double play! Side out! Our turn to bat.

As I grew older, I played a lot of sports. Some of the time my dad coached me. Most of the time not. I know there were times he was proud of me, and there are things I am proud of accomplishing. He was probably beaming with pride when I made the unassisted double play. But I don't remember his reaction, that part of the moment. I wish I could.

I remember the other boys coming over and patting me on the back. I remember feeling lucky and a little scared but not proud. I wasn't ready to swagger or strut. In those days you didn't do dances in the end zone or curtain calls after the home run. You put your head down, went back to the bench, and got ready for what was next. If guys in those days did the kind of celebrating and carrying on like they do now on television, they were sure to get the ultimate insult: they'd be told they were acting like a pussy. I think catching that ball was a decent first step in my not being a pussy, and I wasn't about to ruin it.

CHAPTER 6

Home Team Up to Bat

June 11th, 1945

Dear Wife,

Wake Mills up and tell him you and him got a letter from Daddy. Yes, honey, I am getting mail from you pretty good. I heard about my son—and I love you. I'm glad I've got a son—I just wish I could be with you and him. Did he ride home in our car? Did he want to drive—or didn't he like to drive in a car? I'll bet he'll be wanting to take the car and go courting by the time he is fourteen. Darling, we've got to give him a little different life than either of us had when we were growing up. I've been thinking about how to answer the questions he is going to ask—things like what to tell him when he hears his first bad words and wants to know what it means or repeats it surprisingly. When he hears there is no Santa Claus and begins to wonder. When he wants to know where he came from and things like that. I don't believe in telling a kid too much false stuff like that—and things about boogers and the booger man. Did your mother tell you about things when you were about thirteen years old? I mean about sex and where you came from and stuff? Honey, I want our baby to feel he can talk to us about everything—I want him to feel free to ask us questions—and not be afraid we will scold him, condemn him, and maybe whip him, for asking—or for thinking what it might be. Darling, I was so far away from my family when I was just a tot. I don't remember much about it—but I do know my Mother and Father would be the last persons in the world I would confide in about anything. I want Mills to be close to us—and confide in us about everything. June the fourth was the day that my baby was supposed to be born but that is the day I got word he was already born.

I'm glad we stopped here on Trinidad because if we had not, I probably would still not know that my son was born and my wife is okay. I want my boy to have some advantages we didn't have when we were growing up—and too I want to see that you start enjoying life—and have enough fun and enjoyment out of life to make up for what you missed when you were younger, that is the two things I am living for, to see that my wife has a pleasant life—and my boy an all around advantageable life. And Darling, you can't have a pleasant life working and slaving all the time so you might as well resign the idea that people were made to be slaves of labor because I won't stand for it. After all someone else takes advantage of your labor while you are just completely fatigued from it. When I get home I'm going to do all the worrying about all three of us—you are just going to take it easy—and be my sweet adorable pretty wife. That's the way I want you honey. I can take care of us all three of us. I might not get off to a bang and I will probably have to ask your advice of a lot of things and how to do a lot of things, but I will get around to where I'll have things going pretty smoothly, just like I want them too. Pinch Mills for me.

Love, Charlie

I HAVE NO IDEA when my father lost his idealized fantasy of what life would be like back in Hildebran. Perhaps it came after the third or fourth child. Most likely reality was always waiting for him as part of the times. I don't remember a time when my mother was not working, and at least when I was still living at home, she always seemed to have that quality of weariness that my dad talked about in his letter.

My parents worked hard; both had jobs beyond our home that was also a small farm, collectively earning enough money that we never went to bed hungry and we were always adequately if not stylishly clothed. My mother had a little mantra that she often repeated at the end of the day. With a visible and audible sigh she would say, "Well, I guess I've earned my rest." When she died in 1988, my siblings and I agreed on her epitaph. It reads as follows:

> *Her children are grown,*
> *Her garden is tended,*
> *She has earned her rest.*

The closeness that my father wanted with his child was also a dream not fully realized. The things that got in the way of that are things beyond this story, but I think he did better with me than with any of my other siblings, and not just because of baseball. He tried. He had some talks with me about difficult topics. During my early teens I did a fair amount of hitchhiking around town. He pulled me aside to ask if I knew about or had ever run into, during my hitchhiking, people who were "hamasexuals." He said that if I took enough rides with strangers, I might run into a man that might want to "mess with me." He went on to say that he had known quite a few of them in the army and that for the most part they were gentle and harmless people. He said all I needed to do was to say I was not interested and ask to get out of the car.

His idealized version of the future may have also been impacted by the dark and fearful perception of life held by my mother's mother, the only grandparent I actually knew. She was strong, she was smart, and she mastered her world. She raised ten children, all of whom made real contributions to the community. Yet Grandma Yoder believed and communicated to her grandchildren that the world is a hard and scary place. I understand this as the life she lived, and I do not judge her for it, but one must bear witness to it, in the service of understanding my and my father's lives.

Grandmother was taught that black people were dangerous. Indeed, some of them were literally poisonous. These blacks were known as "blue-gummed niggers," and if one were to bite you, you would die. The absence of blacks in the community allowed this kind of mythology to take hold and grow in my mind.

Jews were an object of ridicule rather than one to fear, mostly having to do with their continuing vigilance for the arrival of the Messiah. I used to wonder what the modern-day wise men would offer as gifts to the true baby Jesus. Gold was still a good bet and maybe television sets and transistor radios.

Rich people also took their lumps. If a person had money, no doubt it came from no good place. No kingdom of heaven for the owners of the local hosiery mills and furniture factories.

I think it is fair to say that in my mother's and my grandmother's minds, anyone who was not family was suspect and flawed, if not actually evil. That was the world that my grandmother believed in and lived. It was the world into which my mother was born and grew up. It was the world into which my father carried—and then moderated—his dreams. But he still had baseball.

∞

Dad was clearly energized by our escape from trouble in the top of the first inning. For our turn at the plate he took up the position of the third-base coach, the most important of the field-manager spots for the team at bat. He clapped his hands enthusiastically, encouraging us with things like "Now's the time ... Show 'em what you can do."

He wore a green baseball-style cap adorned with the John Deere logo, and he held a clipboard used to keep score of the game. The hat and the clipboard were also the focus for the baseball signs he had selected for the game.

I have always been amazed and puzzled when anyone says baseball is boring. If you truly know the game and everything that is happening on the field of play—things that are often silent and unseen, action only in the minds of the participants—then you will find a remarkable complexity that is part of the beauty of the sport. Baseball signs are a big part of this.

Signs are mostly hand signals that guide play, such as the finger signs the catcher puts down between his legs to instruct the pitcher what kind of pitch to throw. But there are many other signs given, usually by the manager, then relayed to the third-base coach, and on to the players. These signs are a series of subtle and sequential movements. The hand touches the arm, leg, touching either on cloth or skin, on the nose, cap, shoe, or sock. It could be hand on skin first, then touch the cap, then back to skin. When correctly interpreted, the batter then obeys the instruction to let a pitch go by or to bunt the ball, sacrificing his own opportunity in order to move a runner forward on the bases. Or the sign could tell a runner to try to steal a base. Maybe hit and run. Double steal. Swing away. It's the sign language of baseball. Being able to read it is part of the skill set.

Dad had little faith in his ten- to twelve-year-olds to correctly interpret complex or subtle signals, so the signs he created for us were rather broad brush. If he wanted the batter to lay off a pitch, forcing the pitcher to throw strikes, he would take off his cap and wave it as if he were cooling his face from the heat of the day. If he laid the clipboard on the ground, that meant for the runner to steal a base. The cap on top of the clipboard on the ground signaled for the batter to bunt. With the signs in mind, our first hitter, Tommy Keller, stepped to the plate. He faced Clayton Lowman, a hard-throwing right-handed pitcher, who along with Paul Fowler was one of the oldest boys on the field. Clayton was good. He threw hard, and three pitches later Tommy walked back to the bench. One out.

My brother, Mills, batted next. He could hit a baseball. After a few pitches just off the plate, one that he let go for a ball, another he fouled softly down the first baseline, he connected and sent a sharp line drive over the head of the second baseman into right field for our first hit and base runner.

We erupted with cheers and chatter. It was the first time that we seemed to have the upper hand. Their shortstop, Roger, came in for a brief chat with Clayton and then ran back out to his position yelling encouragement to his team. "One away! Let's get two with a ground ball ... Go to second!" They picked up their chatter, and the field was alive with the energy and excitement of eighteen boys.

"Fire it in there, Babe ..."

"Throw some smoke ..."

And from our side: "Got a rally now ..."

"Pick out a good one ... Little bingle gets a run ..."

Up next for us was Louie Page, one of the original boys who had talked me into my tearful begging to sign up for the Hickory league. He rode regularly with us to those games that first year. Louie had some of Paul Fowler's knowledge and style at bat. He had his own rituals, and he looked like a baseball player, muscular enough but thin—wiry.

Louie knew about the signs too, so he stepped back from the batter's box to look down the third baseline to see if Coach Charlie was offering up one of his signals. Usually the third hitter in the order is a power hitter and does not bunt another runner along, but I think Louie knew that we would not have a lot of chances to score, so he was willing to sacrifice his at-bat to move Mills down to second. And he knew Billy was up next, our best hope for an early score.

Dad pulled off his cap and waved it around vigorously. This was the don't-swing sign. Clayton put a fastball right down the center of the plate, and like a good soldier Louie watched it go by.

"Steee-rikke one!" bellowed the umpire.

Louie stepped back and again looked down for a sign. Dad took the clipboard and dropped it on the ground beside him. I figured the cap would follow because I knew he wouldn't be telling Mills to steal a base. Their catcher was Elliot Holloway, another boy a year older than our oldest player. Mills had no chance of stealing second with Clayton pitching and Elliot catching.

Louie looked puzzled. I wondered if he was confused about the signs. Then Dad dropped the cap on top of the clipboard. It was the bunt sign. Louie looked down at the ground, took a deep breath, and stepped back in. Clayton called Elliot to the mound. With gloves covering their mouths to hide and muffle conversation, and after many nods and shakes of the head, both boys in unison spit on the ground and returned to their positions.

The next pitch came in hard and high, just the kind of pitch that would be hard to bunt, but Louie got his bat up enough and put down a perfect roller to the third-base side. Herb Livertt fielded it cleanly and threw Louie out at first. Mills moved easily to second. First baseman Punk Raby walked the ball back to his pitcher, and Billy Cline began his walk from the bench to the batter's box.

Another meeting between pitcher and catcher at the mound. No secret what they were talking about.

"You wanna walk him?" Clayton asked.

"No way ... pitch to him."

"I don't wanna walk him ..." Clayton made his decision.

For a moment the field went silent, but with the decision made, each side again lifted their energy and their chatter.

From their side: "Come, Babe ... Come, Babe."

"Set him down ... Blow it by him."

And from our side: "Wait for your pitch, Billy."

"You got him now ... You got him ..."

Billy looked down the third baseline for a sign. None came. He stepped in, tapped the plate, took a few practice swings, and set himself. Clayton took a deep breath and came to the usual stop in the middle of his windup to hold the runner at second. He looked quickly over his shoulder at Mills, turned, and delivered the ball.

Billy connected with the first pitch, a hard fastball just outside of the strike zone but belt high. The ball screamed high in the air toward right field, the short right field, the one that was as short as left field was long, and the one that ended with a sharp slope down an embankment that led to the sewer system. Seventeen boys, all but Billy, held their breath. The right fielder retreated, moving closer and closer to the bank.

"That ball is gone!" someone cried out, and at just that moment, their right fielder, Joe Lynn, known as "Mickey," stumbled backward and disappeared from view. A heartbeat later, the ball followed him out of sight. Our players cheered and leaped to our feet, rushing to home plate to congratulate Billy. He rounded first base and slowed to a trot, following Mills in a humble victory lap around the bases.

Just then Mickey Lynn reappeared at the top of the bank yelling and jumping up and down wildly. At first no one paid him any attention, but then we saw he was holding up a baseball and screaming, "I caught the ball! I caught the ball! He's out! He's out!"

In fact, no one knew if he caught the ball or not. He was the only one down the hill at the time. But he was holding a baseball. Billy continued his path around the bases, as each side rose to the argument, our team unbelieving and angry, their side insistent, and all eyes turned to Melvin Ruggles, the arbiter of disputes.

Mickey, a muscular boy who would later account well for himself as a lineman on the high school football team, winning awards for the Southern District Seven football conference and for Burke County, jogged confidently back to the infield and presented the ball to Ruggles. He took the ball in his hand and studied it for a full minute, an eternity for the rest of us. He walked away from the crowd of players who were now all gathered in the area between the pitcher's mound and first base. He held up his hand and motioned for us to stay there and not follow him.

Ruggles then called Paul Fowler and Dad over, and with their backs turned to us, they discussed the situation calmly. One could have believed they were talking about the weather. Then they took a short walk out to right field and stood there looking down at the area where Mickey said he caught the ball. Finally Ruggles motioned for everyone to come out to the edge of the bank, and we all stood there looking over the edge, down into the sewer. We stood there for just a moment without anyone speaking.

Ruggles then turned to address the teams. "Just like the ball that Paul hit in the top of the inning, we did not discuss any ground rules about what to do in this kind of situation. So it will have to be my judgment." He paused for any reactions. No one spoke.

Ruggles looked down at the ball. Then he held it up for all to see. "This could be the ball that was hit. It looks like the ball we were using. If it is, only two things are possible. One, he caught it, because if it is the ball and he didn't catch it, he would not have had time to have run it down and get back up the bank that fast. And if he didn't catch it, it would be wet. Two, the other possibility is that he's lying and took a ball out of his pocket that looks like our ball."

Ruggles walked a few steps away back toward the infield. He put his cap back on his head, replaced his facemask, and barked, "I'm not ready to call him a liar. The batter is out! The inning is over! Charlie, get your boys back out on the field. Batter up!"

⌘

My dad accepted Ruggles's decision without comment or argument. With a wave of his clipboard and a tug on his John Deere hat, he motioned for us to get back to the game. As we broke into a slow jog back to the bench to get our gloves, someone at the back of the group whispered, loud enough for all to hear, "That ball is in the sewer, and everybody knows it."

Dad turned around, unsure who said it, but definite in his response. "Now, listen. I won't put up with griping about the umpire. The call has been made. Now get back out there, and let's play some ball."

I look back on that now and take note of his letter of June 11. It's not the same as "there is no Santa" or his thoughts about the bogeyman, but there is a theme here. The world is not always fair, and things are not always done right, so get used to things not being perfect. Blame gets you nowhere. Face the truth. Deal with it. Play ball. Get your head back in the game, and quit your whining.

Ruggles's decision also had a certain symmetry. In any other ballpark with a normal left field, Paul Fowler's ball would have been a long home run. In any other ballpark with a normal right field, Mickey Lynn might have had a chance to catch what could have been just Billy's long fly ball. I think Dad knew that. The rules were not perfect, but one could argue that they were applied fairly after all. At least there were rules to guide the play, even if it did take the judgment of people to make them fair.

CHAPTER 7

Keeping Your Cool

June 17th, 1945

Dear Charlotte,

How is my wife and little old Mills today? I'm thinking of you both—Gee Honey, I got two people now—it's wonderful but hard to realize. I remember one year ago to date—I was looking forward to seeing you the next day—I had only one people then—but I sure did love that one. I just had one people the last time I saw you too—but there was a maybe, and I left you with having just one people and a maybe. I started out on the Atlantic Ocean riding a small Liberty Ship, the S.S. Betty Zane and was out a few days and had ship trouble, so the Betty Zane left the convoy and pulled in to Bermuda—I had some hopes of hearing from my one people while I was back to Bermuda—in a few days we sailed again on the Betty Zane—which was beginning to seem like a bad luck ship and guys who were superstitious were afraid.

The Betty Zane sailed the big ocean alone, unescorted, for several days—I was thinking of my one people day in and day out—and wondering if there were really going to be two. We had plenty of reading material on the ship and at night below decks they tried to hold some kinds of programs to keep guys minds occupied. Some nights they would have bingo games, some nights they would try to teach some Italian language, for after we got under way we were told where we were going. They rigged up a couple of stage shows a couple of nights out of volunteers who had talent for something entertaining. I didn't follow the routine with the troops though—I figured it would be better to get a steady working detail, so I got a job with the ships crew baking bread at nights—that way I could prowl around the ship at night when the decks were not so crowded with troops, and sort a had a free hand around there. Some of the boys would let me steer the ship late at night when the Captain and First Mate were asleep. That way the trip was not so tiresome and monotonous—and when we would run into a storm or something that would frighten the troops on board—I would be hanging around with the ships crew and they didn't get excited they had been through it so much they just laughed and didn't give a dern, so being around them I didn't get frightened. I kept trusting that my one people would be okay and I would hear from you when I reached my destination, and I kept hoping that there would really be two of you too.

From time to time there would be rumors of enemy submarines, and I could not figure out why we alone were never attacked. After some days we met up with another convoy. Two subs were sighted by this convoy and driven away by destroyer escorts. We traveled with this convoy to Africa, there they left us, our troops officers had led us to believe that in the Mediterranean there would be air attacks and subs, but all the crew seemed to worry about was running into floating water mines. We pulled into Naples harbor and sat there a couple of days before debarking. After debarking we went to Caserta. Living conditions were rough there and we were kept on the alert for action at all times. This is where I got a bunch of letters and packages from my one people and was assured that there were going to be two of you, well, I figured thats natural, there should be two of you, why not? Thats what I want, and I could easily picture my having two people in this world, in the future of course.

They separated us there, some went to the fighting front, some went different places, and I went to Pomigliano and was assigned to the 28th

T. C Sq. The outfit's planes were flying supplies to Czechoslovakia and carrying their wounded out of hot spots. At this time I was getting mail pretty much regular from my one people and was beginning to worry about you having to suffer the birth of a child. Pomigliano was a small city about the size of Hickory—it was torn all to h— from fighting there and the people were poverty stricken. Did you ever receive a Yank Magazine I sent you from there: Our planes would also fly supplies to our own fighting fronts and to France, and they would sometimes drop paratroopers.

We were not far from Naples and I went there a few times. Naples was also torn up by fighting there and was bombed pretty much. The people seemed to have access to money but no materials and there was a great inflation. G.I.s could sell anything they had for alarming prices—food, clothing, cigarettes, candy, soap, anything. $20 for a carton of cigarettes—$30 to $50 for a ten pound batch of sugar, and any price you ask for garments. About the only thing they had to sell to G.I.s were wines and women. There was a wave of prostitution so heavy G.I.s couldn't walk ten yards without a half dozen kids trying to drag them somewhere to a prostitute. Because of this, the Army had placed all places off limits except through the main streets. MPs picked up all G.I.s that were seen going down an alley off the main streets, they were all off limits to service men. Naples had a population of about one million.

I was still getting pretty regular mail from my one people and am worrying more and more about her having to give birth to a child.

In the closing part of the war in Italy, our planes took part in the Battle of the Apennines, and the Po Valley. Some of us moved up closer to service the planes. I got two battle stars for the participating of the Apennines and Po Valley. Now my chief worry was my wife, will she be okay after the birth of the baby. The last ship I was on was the U.S.S. Richardson. I am now in Trinidad Island and found out my baby is born and you are okay and now I have two people in this world.

The worrying about you being okay more or less took the place in my mind away from thinking about really having a baby, worrying about you being okay, now I can realize that you are okay and it's a great relaxation, but its hard to realize that I have got two people. I have got two people in this world, though, and I am proud. I love my two people too. And I wish I could be closer to them.

Love,
Charlie

I HAVE READ DAD'S June 17 letter many times. It is the most informative one about his war experience and one that I believe may be understated. Men writing back home were known to leave out things that would frighten and worry loved ones. I think he had a lot more to say about his involvement in the Po Valley. The sum total of his writing seems to suggest he never fired a weapon in anger and was never shot at, but I think he saw the horror of war, at least in the injured troops on the planes coming back from the battle zones.

Perhaps his war experiences contributed to a sense of perspective that I eventually knew him to have. Beyond the keeping of a cool head when umpires made calls that went the wrong way for him, he always seemed to have the attitude that no matter what happened the world would keep on turning and things would somehow work out. I recall conversations with him about politics and history, events as notable as the Kennedy assassination, and days as ordinary as a rained-out ball game. To him few things were as much a crisis as others thought. Of course I couldn't agree with him when my baseball games were rained out.

Another feature of Dad's character showed during an incident when I was a little older. Dad and I stood on the sidelines of the football field with a group of men watching the high school team practice. The team featured a star halfback named Bobby Ledford. To the younger boys of the community Bobby was a god, or at least a superhero. As the team came off the field, one of the men watching made some sort of comment to the players. Bobby took offense. It may have been something about a lack of hustle during practice, something like that. Bobby and some of the men barked back and forth at each other.

I don't remember anything else about what was said, but that night at home my siblings and I interpreted the situation as "Dad almost got into a fight with Bobby Ledford."

"Dad, you better be careful; he could kill you," one of us said out loud.

Dad sat straight up from his lounge chair where he was reading the *Hickory Daily Record*. He didn't get up from the chair, his feet stayed in place on the footstool, but he crunched the paper down in his lap and glared at us, letting out a sarcastic laugh.

"What! Bobby Ledford? You think that I'm afraid … I'm not afraid of any Bobby … Ledford!"

He opened and closed his mouth several more times as if looking for something else to say but added nothing. He lay back down on the lounge chair, raised and straightened the newspaper with a flourish, and muttered one more time, "Bobby … Ledford."

With all he went through as a child and what he must have seen in the war, I now understand what a small problem Bobby Ledford must have seemed.

∞

To say that my father had a things-will-all-be-okay approach to life is not to say he did not want to win the baseball game. Before Billy took the mound again to pitch in the top of the second, he called Billy over, faced him directly, and placed a soft hand on each of Billy's shoulders.

"That call by the ump is just the kind of thing you have to shake off. So shake it off, concentrate on your pitching, and get out there and get the job done."

I could see that Billy first tried to avoid eye contact with Dad, likely out of his anger and disappointment in the call going against him and losing what was obviously a home run. Then he took a deep breath, looked his coach in the eye, and said calmly, "Got it."

A palpable atmosphere of serious-mindedness and determination had now set in on both sides. You could see it in the stern and quiet looks on everyone's faces. No one joked around or made small talk. It took a few moments for anyone to begin the chatter. The controversial calls by the umpire, the missed opportunities for each team, led all in turn to assume an attitude that was all-business. A bright sun beat down on the field. Even those at rest broke a sweat as they shaded their eyes from the glare.

It was the second inning. No score. First batter up for them was Clayton Lowman, their pitcher. Clayton stepped into the batter's box. Billy stared him down for a time longer than usual, and just before Billy started his windup, Clayton motioned to Ruggles for a time-out. Billy threw the pitch anyway, but the time-out was granted. No pitch.

Billy stared down at him again. Clayton again motioned for time to be called. Ruggles ripped off his protective facemask and with a dramatic gesture marched out a few steps between home plate and the pitcher's mound and delivered a lecture. "Right now! The games you two are playing will stop. Or you can take a seat. That's it!" Ruggles took a step toward one bench and then the other, making it clear to each in turn. "It's time to stop the monkey business and play ball!"

The players returned to their respective spots, Billy on the mound ready to go, Clayton scratching out a small trench in the front of the batter's box with his front foot. Billy delivered a hard, high fastball, just in the strike zone.

"Steeeriike one!"

Druey fired the ball back to Billy. "Hey, Babe ... Hum, Babe ... Got it goin' now!" Billy wasted no time and threw another fastball, toward the outside of the plate and low in the strike zone.

"Steeeriike two!"

Clayton stepped quickly out of the box, obviously not liking the call, but he stopped short of showing open complaint. He took the bat and tapped his shoes as if knocking mud off of baseball spikes, despite the fact that he wore only flat-soled sneakers.

The chatter from the infielders grew. "Hey, Babe! Hey, Babe! One more now ... One more now. Right in there now ... You the man!"

Billy's third pitch was a little high and a little inside of the zone, but with two strikes on him Clayton could not hold back. He swung hard, but his bat found only air.

"Steeeriike three!" bellowed Ruggles, and with a pump of his right fist he indicated the batter was out. Face red and neck veins bulging, Clayton walked quickly back to the bench. Neither player looked at the other. Emotions were high, but the game faces were set. There would be no losing control. Too much was at stake.

Next up was Elliot Holloway, who looked thin from a distance but up close was all muscle, toned and strong. When older he would play center on the high school football team next to Mickey Lynn at guard.

Billy was done with staring down the other side. He delivered his first pitch without delay, starting with a slow curveball that set Elliot off balance. A weak swing found just a nick of the ball, and it squibbed softly away on the ground toward first base. Foul ball. Strike one.

Working fast now, Billy took a little speed off of his best fastball, and it came to the plate looking big and fat. Elliot misjudged the speed and swung too early, hitting the ball squarely but pulling it foul down the third baseline. Strike two.

The third pitch came to Elliot high, hard, and fast and was past him before he could offer even a token swing.

"Steeriike three!" The second batter of the inning took the long walk back to the bench.

Norman Bess, another boy big for his age, tall and muscular, walked slowly to home plate. He swung three bats to warm up. He took extra time before stepping into the box, first throwing away one bat, continuing to swing the remaining two, and then finally disposed of the second one before letting out a long grunting sound. "Uuuunnnhhhhhhh!" Then he took his place, ready to hit.

After Billy had disposed of the first two batters so efficiently, Dad could see that the rest of us were just standing around, the chatter gone and no one looking ready to play. He jumped to his feet and shouted a scolding command for us to get ready. "We need all of you to get your heads in the game!"

Norman let the first pitch go by. "Steeeriike one!" trumpeted Ruggles.

Staying in the box but holding up his hand for time and tapping the ground hard with his bat, Norman looked off balance, not ready. Ruggles immediately chimed, "Play ball," and pointed to Billy, clearly motioning for him to go ahead with the next pitch, making it clear he was fed up with all the posturing and delaying.

Billy came this time with another long, lazy, slow curveball. Norman swung, letting out another long grunt. "Uuuunnnnhhhh!" He missed the ball by a foot and spun around twice before dropping the bat at his feet in frustration. Ruggles glared at him. He picked up the bat promptly and readied himself.

Our infield raised the level of chatter another notch. I felt as if I were surrounded by sound, even in this open field. I practically screamed my contribution. I wiped sweat from my forehead with my glove. I spit as I saw Clayton and Roger do. I pounded my fist into my glove and almost fell forward before taking a deep breath and calming myself down, planting my feet still and solidly on the ground, ready for the next pitch.

There had been eight pitches and eight strikes. The other team grew as quiet as a church choir during prayer. I think it was the point they figured out what they were up against in Billy Cline. The looks on their faces said one thing: "This guy is good." I know this was the point that I figured out what I was involved in—more than a game, some kind of connectedness I had never felt before.

This last pitch of this half inning came in hard and low in the strike zone and passed over the inside corner of the plate. It was a perfect pitch. Norman saw he could not catch up to it and could not shift his stance to reach it. He gave a futile and weak wave of the bat, not even a real attempt to make contact. He didn't wait to hear Ruggles's call before starting his walk back.

All through their at-bat, Dad was mostly quiet and sat still and composed on the bench. But when Ruggles called the third strike, he leaped to his feet, holding his cap in his hand, bouncing up and down and waving wildly for his players to get off the field and up to bat.

"Okaaaayy! Pick it up! Get in here … Run—don't walk! Lambert, you're up first! Icard, you're next! Rudisill … Rudisill, time to show me something! Let's get some hits!"

I ran in from second base, barely able to make myself sit down on the bench as we were supposed to do. I wanted to scream or dance or sing or just do something to let the world know that "Hey! I am here! I am on this team! I'm a part of this, with these gods, with these superheroes, and it's me. I can do this—me! I'm in the game!"

CHAPTER 8

Family Matters

July 12, 1945

Dear Charlotte,

Hey Darling—I guess my baby should be a sweet baby—after all look who his mother is. How could he be anything but sweet? His mother is about the sweetest wife I ever had—I like her too.

So Dr. Palmer thinks old chip is okay and doing alright—well, what does Chip think of Dr. Palmer—I'll bet he don't like Mrs. Justice for sticking him with her old needle. Did he bawl when she vaccinated him? Did she notice that his name was Mills—tell her that we named him after Mills Home if you wish?

Honey your Mother and Dad are getting old, and their actions are going to be somewhat selfish and hard to reason with—and they are going to drive you—but what they will be driving you for is not what they really want—and if you let them drive you in that direction they will drive you to be as old as they are. So what they really want is an enlightenment from burdens etc. And to hear some one else give the alibis and excuses to enlighten that burden. They might never admit that that is what they want, they might just keep on saying so and so is wrong—and this and that has to be done—and has to be done in a particular way—but as long as you don't do it—or don't let them do it—they can be enlightened by the fact that you agree with their real inner thoughts and by the fact that if wrong was done you done it, not them. You can't reason with them by bucking them and fussing and arguing against them—that will create a grudge and make them think the whole world has turned them down when they got old. And they will be very unhappy. A little smiling, laughing, and chatter, and teasing will do the trick. That's what they want, a little enlightenment although it may not seem that way—it might seem that they want nothing but real old hard grinding. You and your mother have always been too serious about getting out of bed in the morning and that kind of stuff. They are getting old and that one think you aren't going to be able to do anything about—and there will be lots of things that you will not be able to help—but you can enlighten things by a little teasing, chatter and laughing and giving alibis for them. For example, when your Mother starts walking the floor and acting mad or something because you don't get up or something—then tease her, talk to her, tell her to take it easy that life is not so dern important—that you only live once and all kind of stuff like that—keep talking like that to her every time she acts that way or pouts or gets stubborn—make her think life is not so dreadful—when something might should be done and its hard for her to do—tell her just the heck with it the sun will shine tomorrow even if its not done. When she wants you to do something, or wants to do something herself that you don't want to do or want her to do give her a reason for not doing it. You see honey, you can't let them run your life now, because it will be too much of a strain on you—and the way they will drive you is not what they want anyway—so you have to control and run their lives—and thats about the only way to do it.

The hard truth is that she loves all the other brothers and sisters just as much as she done you enspite of how much you have done for her and how little they have done. So what you really do or don't do as far as work, getting out of bed, and things like that are concerned don't really matter—thats been proven and should be very obvious. What will matter from here on out will be cheering her a little, keeping her company, and talking to her—the contrast between words and actions are argued, but strangely enough, words have the most effect with people. So honey don't work yourself to death, take it easy if you can't hire someone to keep enough wood cut for this winter, buy coal. Don't hesitate to spend the money you get from the government, or what you have already saved either.

Stay with your Mother and Father honey, and take care of them, but do it in your way—don't let them run your life. You are a pretty good old wife honey and I will be glad when I can get to come home to live with you. We will take care of the old folks and enjoy living too, by granny we will. I'm going to get over my tongue tiredness around your Mother too, I'm going to talk to her and we'll make her feel good—and we'll enjoy life too. I'll talk her into living easy and getting by just as good. And me and my wife are going to have a good time—and I got a little old Chip too—he will be included in the deal also.

Love,
Charlie

I WISH I HAD the letter my mother wrote that inspired my dad's advice about handling her parents' demands. Even without it, I find the letter informative about life in that time and place. Dad's letter is consistent with my memory of my grandmother: a hardworking, stern woman. My grandfather died just after my first birthday.

I doubt that his advice was helpful to Mother. His thoughts of an easy life did not come true. He worked hard to run our small farm while keeping his job at the bakery. I can only imagine how Grandmother would have reacted if he or my mother ever told her to lighten up a little and smell the roses. She was born in the South in the shadow of the Civil War, and she and my grandfather scratched out a self-sufficient living on sixty acres of rocky soil, raised ten children who lived to adulthood, and buried two more who did not survive the dangers of the early 1900s. I think "live in the moment" or "consider the lilies of the field" would have been quite foreign to her experience of life.

Dad's advice, of course, is more about him. How he developed this live-for-the-easy-life point of view, however, is a mystery to me. Perhaps the Mills Home orphanage, for which my brother was named, gave him some nurture and structure beyond his early childhood and the pain of his losses. I know the orphanage was one place he learned about games.

Maybe the army showed him other ways to play. I know that a few years before the second-greatest game he and my mother had a falling-out about his poker playing with some friends. Whether this was harmless penny poker or a risk to losing necessary bread money I don't know, but evidently this was the issue. The answer may be unimportant to this story; it may be unknowable. But Dad did have a nickname: Two-Pair Charlie. He was well enough known in those circles. It's one piece of the puzzle of his character, something that I rather admire, a fun and perhaps risk-taking side of him.

Nevertheless, we never went to bed hungry, and while we were a family of modest means, I never lacked for anything I needed. And I learned to love games as my father did. Back to the game.

❧

Druey Lambert ran his few steps to the batter's box. He played with energy but also had a calm, composed manner, even when all around him were whooping it up with the chatter.

"Let's get it goin' now!"

"Need some runs … Need some runs …"

Our side was pumped up and confident after Billy set their side down so convincingly in the top half of the inning. The other team seemed deflated, cautious. No one on their side stepped forward to lift the energy level. But this didn't matter to Clayton. He stood on the mound with a dark determination showing on his face. He was every bit as calm as his batting opponent and fired the first pitch with speed he had not shown us before.

"Steeeeeeeriiiiiiiiiike one." Ruggles called this one with a kind of singsong cadence as if to give due admiration for the quality of the effort. Having reestablished his authority and control, he seemed to hold forth with a bit of showmanship at this point in the game. Ruggles's demeanor was not one of an anonymous participant. He was part of the day's story. Not a tall man, he had to look up to the faces of some of these thirteen- and fourteen-year-olds. But no one looked down on him.

Druey tapped the ground with his bat, his only offering of ritual, and waited for the next pitch. It bounced in the dirt near his feet for ball one. The catcher, Elliot, scooped it up effortlessly on one hop and fired it back to his pitcher. Druey tapped. Clayton scowled. Clayton fired the next pitch.

"Steeeeeeerrrrriiiiiiiike two!" Ruggles's singing call of the pitch seemed to energize our opponents. They exploded with chatter.

"Hey, hey, hey, Babe, whaddayousay!"

"He's just lookin' … He's yours!"

The only reaction I saw from Druey was an obvious widening of his eyes and a brief glance up, but that said a lot. Just as Billy had raised his game, Clayton seemed to do the same. Druey's expression said, "This guy's better than I thought."

Druey stepped back in the box and waved his bat with renewed energy. The next pitch came hot, and the swing connected but too much under the ball. The ball soared high into the air straight above home plate. I remember how calmly Elliot stood his ground as he ripped off his face mask, threw it a safe distance away so as to not trip over it, and watched and waited for the ball to return to earth. He didn't stagger around or shuffle his feet as I would have done. He just waited as the ball fell, lower and lower. Ruggles too had removed his face protector but held it in his hand as he moved away to give the fielder room. Druey reluctantly retreated, hoping that the ball might drift back out of play, but Elliot stood motionless, gloved hand extended upward, other hand on his hip. The ball fell softly into his catcher's mitt.

"Batter's out!" Ruggles announced, needlessly. With no expression or reaction Druey walked back to the bench and began putting on his protective gear for when it was time for him to take the field.

Elliot fired the ball down to Herb at third base. He caught it with a sharp snap of his glove and continued the ritual that follows each out if there are no runners on base. Catcher throws to third, he in turn throws to second base, then to shortstop, then on to the first baseman, who walks the ball a few steps closer to the pitcher before tossing it softly back to him. The first time I saw this around-the-horn exercise, I asked Dad about it, and he explained, "It keeps the fielders warmed up and busy, keeps their heads in the game when they don't have anything else to do."

The other team was clearly back in the game. Clayton stood tall on the mound ready to pitch to Ted Icard even before his opponent was ready. Ted held up one hand to Ruggles asking for more time to settle into the batter's box. Ruggles raised both hands for only a second and then gave the play-ball command. Even this brief pause seemed to frustrate Clayton, who was ready to go, and he stepped back off the mound, pounded the ball into his glove, and glared at Ted. I guess his frustration this time got the better of him because when he did deliver the first pitch, it sailed inside and hit Ted square in the middle of the back as he twisted away, squirming unsuccessfully to get out of the way of the ball.

Being hit with a baseball is not fun, but unless it hits you in the head, it's not that dangerous. Yet it's always a matter of pride. It can feel like a whipping even if there is no injury. Players don't like to look hurt, and there's an unspoken rule that you don't rub or otherwise call attention to the place the ball hit you. And there is the matter of what the pitcher intended. The pitcher's words or body language can convey an "Oops, I'm sorry" or "That's what you get for messin' with me."

Clayton showed no remorse, and Ted dropped his bat to the ground and glared back at Clayton. Ruggles jumped in. "Batter, take your base." Ted did not move. Clayton returned his stare.

"Batter, take your base, or take your seat!" bellowed Ruggles, thus ending the standoff.

Ted trotted down to first base, and the two opponents turned their eyes away from the other. Roger ran in from shortstop to settle his pitcher. Dad called time-out and ran quickly to check on Ted. I was not close enough to hear the conversation, but it looked like Dad asked if he needed to look at where the ball hit. Ted was having none it. He kept the rule. He was not hurt. No one needed to rub his back. Leave him alone. He could take care of himself. If anything else needed to be done, he had it covered. Dad made no attempt to smile, joke, or tease Ted out of his mood.

I don't really know what was said or what was going on in Ted's mind. Maybe my encounter with him on the playground earlier that year had something to do with my interpretation of the events. But I would not want to hit Ted Icard with a baseball.

Clayton walked a few steps away toward third base to refocus his thoughts and then stepped quickly back to the pitcher's mound to face the next batter, Jerry Rudisill, our first baseman. Jerry was much taller and clearly more physically mature than the rest of the boys in our class at school. He even had the start of sideburns. Maybe he missed a year of school; I didn't know his story.

Jerry had his own batting ritual. He took a deep, deep breath and pumped his arms and elbows like a chicken trying to fly. He looked down at Dad in the coaching box and saw the clipboard and hat on the ground, the sign for a bunt. I could see the air go out of him. He wanted to hit the ball, not sacrifice, but he dutifully squared around and waited for the first pitch.

Whether or not the other team had figured out Dad's signal for the bunt, I'm not sure, but their infielders responded right away, third baseman charging in from third, the first baseman taking a few steps in closer to home plate, and the second baseman moving toward first to cover if needed. These were the classic defensive adjustments to defend against the bunt.

The first pitch came slow and low in the strike zone, a sweeping curveball that Jerry poked at weakly and missed. Dad immediately picked up his cap and clipboard, figuring out that neither Jerry's heart nor his skill were right for bunting. The next two pitches went high and outside the strike zone. Two balls, one strike. Our spirits picked up, and chatter rang out.

"Got him now, Jerry; got him goin'!"

"Take him deep, big guy; take him deep!"

No pitcher wants to go to a three balls and one strike count, so a two and one in favor of the batter is a *hitter's count*. The pitcher will often take a little off the pitch to make sure it is a strike, so it's usually a good pitch to hit. This one came to the plate slow and fat, right across the plate. Jerry took a big cut and lined it foul just out of play down the third baseline. You could see the frustration of a missed opportunity on Jerry's face. Two balls, two strikes.

Spirit and momentum seemed to change with every pitch. The next one was no exception. Clayton gave him another sweeping curve that started out high and inside but dropped into the strike zone at the last moment.

"Striiiike thrreeeeeeeeee, you're out!" trumpeted Ruggles, hamming it up with a double pump of his right hand and keeping it stretched out longer than usual with his fist wiggling back and forth for more dramatic effect. Ruggles continued to be an actor in the drama.

Next up was Tommy Parham, and this was a special problem for me because I was up next. If Tommy got on base, I would be faced with the possibility—no, the certainty—of making the last out of the inning. I'd be the goat. The rally stopper. The choker. It was the one time that day I hoped my teammate would make an out.

Tommy batted left-handed and had the smooth-move rituals polished to a shine. Hitch the pants. Tug on the bill of the cap. Pull the bat around in a slow warm-up swing with just his right hand holding on to it as if to say, "I'll take you with one hand." Then he would crouch, put both hands on the bat, and nod his head confidently, as if to add, "Come on in here. I'm right here, and we are goin' long."

But Clayton was ready too. He was in his own zone of effort where everything was working, and to everyone's surprise he threw another long, lazy curveball. It seemed to almost stop in midair and wait for Tommy to crush it, but the bat struck empty space a foot above the ball as it dipped as if it had fallen off a table. A half-smile, half-smirk flashed across Clayton's face as he caught the ball back from the catcher.

"Hum, Babe, hum, Babe, you got it workin' now!"

"Send him home with the mail, home with the mail!"

Clayton threw again, this time a fastball that Tommy took for strike two right down the middle of the zone. Tommy watched it all the way into the glove. He began to nod again and stepped out of the batter's box. He tapped his feet with the bat, knocking imaginary mud from nonexistent spikes. He stepped in again, shortened his ritual by half, and left off the nodding. Clayton took a quick look toward first to hold Ted from stealing and then fired. Tommy caught the pitch firmly and sent a sharp ground ball into right field for a single. Ted stopped on second, and I realized I was up to bat. Two men on. Two out. No score. And it was my turn.

I remember clearly all that led up to put me in this predicament, but I don't really remember much about taking my place to face Clayton that first time. What happened next came so fast it took me a few extra moments to figure it all out. As Clayton delivered a fastball and I stood still with the bat on my shoulder as the ball came in for a strike, Ted Icard broke for third. Dad had put on the steal sign.

Elliot caught the ball cleanly and gunned it true to Herb at third. The ball was there a step ahead of Ted, who was easily tagged out. I was spared the shame of making the third out. Thanks, Dad.

Dad came halfway down the third baseline waving his arm like a speedway flagman while he shouted encouragement to all of us. "That's okay! That's okay! Got to take a chance to get somethin' done. We're okay. We're good. Get back out there. Go get 'em!"

Two innings in the books. No score.

CHAPTER 9

Words and the Language of Baseball

August 3rd, 1945

Dear Charlotte,

Okay, you can go to the show this afternoon if Chip doesn't care. Tell me about the show and what Chip done about you going. Was he pretty glad to see you when you got back? Maybe he would take a notion to run up about Valdese and look up those little girls who were in the maternity ward with him, while you are gone to the show—so you better tell his grandma to keep a pretty close eye on him and not let him get started out toward Hildebran.

Out with other girls? You mean out with other women; you are a woman now lady, and you have got an old man and a little bambino to your credit. Yeah, I think a lot of marriages break up for the very reason that they make each other stick around with each other too close, too much. If couples see too much too long of each other it pretty much kills the appreciation for each other. Especially so if they are forced by the other one to stick around all the time. If one wants to get away from the other, and the other forces him, or her, to stay regardless of what the one might possible do while away—it is by far worse to make one stay, because that will kill the appreciation of being together—fast!!

A free hand is absolutely necessary in a successful marriage—even so if one wants to go too much and all the time, because if one does the chances are that one doesn't love the other one anyway, or at least that one is not satisfied being with the other one, and forcing that one to stay—sure as H—won't make the one love the other one, or satisfy one.

Anything that one is forced to do against their wish can positively not be appreciated. Even when couples love each other as much as you and I do—it is still best to go separately pretty much frequently, so that the appreciation of being together will be greater when we really are together. However we haven't been together enough yet—we certainly were not together enough during our courtship enspite of the numbers of years it was; and we might find problems fronting us yet because of that but we can solve them. I expect the problems, but I don't know what their nature will be; and I want you to expect them too. If we are expecting them, we can reason with them and solve them better and faster. Also by expecting them we can avoid words like "well, what did you marry me for" and "if I had known that I wouldn't have married you" which are very cutting words. We must always think before we speak, honey, because due to the fact that we were not together enough we are most likely to find out things we didn't know about each other enspite of how well we thought we knew each other. The truth is—we know very little about each other, and all we did know was that we were in love with each other, and that was a dead certain fact. You realize all that too, don't you darling? Also about thinking before we speak—we are both very sensitive to words, aren't we?

There are a lot of Brazilian kids working out here at the base—and right now there are about 12–15 hanging around me—they can't read English though, so I don't think they know what is in this letter. They want to know how much my watch cost, and are asking questions about it which I can't understand. One of them wanted to buy it for $10 but when I told him it cost $75 he didn't say any more about buying it. I figured it would get rid of him quicker than telling him I would not sell it for any price. Funny thing is that these people don't have money galore like the Italians did, and there is no black market where you can get unearthly prices of cigarettes, et. cetra. However, this is a much richer country than Italy—in fact, their dollar is worth more than *ours. They speak the Portuguese language which has a lot of words the same as Italian, but they can't understand Italian as a whole.*

I got your letters today of July 29 and 30 and I also got one from Dorcas. I don't think shoes are rationed down here but they don't have any in the PX, however, I'll try to get some in town—but I don't know if I can—maybe. You can put the money in the Valdese bank if you want to honey—it is your money.

Yes honey we can get along together and have a good time when I get home okay—I know we can do that—but what is worrying me is what the heck I am going to do to make us a living. Hope we don't have to sell old Chip or something.

Love,
Charlie

WRITTEN ON AUGUST 3, 1945, this letter certainly did not make it back home to Mother before August 6, the day the atomic bomb fell on Hiroshima, essentially ending the Pacific War. In the letters Dad said nothing about what he was doing in Brazil, but we ultimately learned he was preparing to be a part of the force that would have invaded Japan. He never spoke of his actual role or training activities. He kept his letters focused on what was going on back home and what kind of life he and Mother would share.

As far as his advice about closeness and distance in relationships, he ended up being right about this as a problem for them. They went through at least one period of real struggle. In my early teens, my siblings and I carried messages between them because even though we all stayed together in a rather small house, they seldom spoke directly to each other.

His advice in the letter might have been more helpful in a time and place where the labor of clothing and feeding a family was less overwhelming, in a family with more options for how they spent their hours. His vision in the letter was not the life to which he returned after the war. I think Mother found him to be the grasshopper to her ant.

There were other sources of stress. After Grandmother died, Mother and her brothers and sisters found themselves in a feud about how to divide up the sixty acres of land they all owned collectively. They split up into three warring groups. Some did not speak to each other for years. I remember there was a big meeting of Mother and her siblings to which Dad was not invited. There was some scheme about getting a walkie-talkie to hide under the couch where the meeting was held, so Dad could hear what was going on.

My parents eventually got something good going again between them, after the children were launched. In the years before Mother's death in 1988, during one of my visits home, I watched them play a game, a kind of hide-and-seek, in the house when she returned from shopping. Dad hid, and Mother walked around, in and out of rooms, calling out, "Okay, come on now; I know you're here somewhere." She checked the usual closets then under the beds, and this time she found him scrunched down in a small space behind a couch. "How'd you get down there?" They laughed and hugged.

They were working out the togetherness, the closeness, and the distance, without the actual words. It was a clear answer to the questions "Did you miss me" and "Do you really want me around enough to come looking for me?"

Two scoreless innings were now recorded in the scorebook. The scorebook itself was magical to me, a source of endless fascination. The baseball scorebook is a template, a structure on which to write the story of the game in a language unique and perfect to its function. The pages of the scorebook are laid out as a graph of sorts with the list of players on one axis and each inning along the other. Each defensive position on the field is assigned a number. So if the ball is hit on the ground to the shortstop, designated as the number six, and if the shortstop is able to successfully throw the ball to get the runner out at first, the out is scored as 6–3, with three being the number for the first baseman. If the batter hit a fly ball caught by the left fielder, the out would be recorded as F-7. Base hits are recorded with various minus or plus signs, with a home run marked with +++, the glorious triple plus sign. The letter *K* signifies that the batter struck out.

In the ensuing years there were many scorebooks representing many games around the house, mostly from games after the formal leagues were established in Hildebran. I relished reading them as true and personal history books. Alas, the book of the second-greatest game has been lost, tossed out I suppose with my collection of baseball cards. I have joked that if I had kept up with my Honus Wagner and Nap Lajoie cards I could sell them into a comfortable retirement. In truth I do mourn them as a real loss.

From the scorebook one can recreate the action, the play-by-play of a game. The scorebook is also the official record from which baseball's seemingly infinite categories of statistics are drawn: batting averages, fielding averages, most runs batted in by a right-handed redheaded Italian second baseman under thirty years old in games played in June won by the visiting team when pitching a left-handed rookie.

I pored over these kinds of records and statistics. I'm sure I never would have mastered long division if I had not needed to calculate Gil Hodges's batting average. One of my summer joys was waiting for the *Hickory Daily Record*, the afternoon newspaper that came sometime around two o'clock. I would turn to the sports page to find the box scores of the previous night's games. Armed with my understanding of the columns of times at bat, runs, hits, errors, and such, I would reconstruct the Brooklyn Dodgers' game. With a glance at my favorite players' stats from the night before I would update their batting averages in my head.

∞

"Batter up!" Ruggles moved the game forward.

Mickey Lynn stepped up to the plate. Football was his best game, but he yielded nothing in any game. Not the tallest player on the field, he crouched low to make his strike zone—just under the armpits to the knees—even smaller. The first two pitches, fastballs, came in high. Two balls, no strikes. Druey called time-out for a quick trip to the mound to talk to his pitcher.

Billy's next pitch floated slowly to the plate. He and Druey calculated that rather than give up a walk they would challenge him with an Eephus pitch. The pitch comes slow, fat, and begging to be hit and sometimes catches the batter off guard. The awkward swing that results can lead to an easy grounder or pop-up or at the least a strike.

Mickey saw the ball inching to the plate, hanging in the air, juicy as a watermelon. He gave a mighty swing and bounced the ball on one hop back to Billy. Billy made the easy toss to first before Mickey was halfway down the baseline. The scorebook showed 1–3 for Mickey's efforts.

"You got 'im, Babe!" chirped the infielders as the ball then traveled from the first baseman to me at second. I passed it on to the shortstop, who then lobbed it to my brother, Mills, at third where he walked the ball a few steps back toward the pitcher's mound and completed the round-the-horn ritual with a soft underhanded toss to Billy.

Next up was Terry Smith, Roger's brother, their youngest player at eleven years old. He stood in bravely, wiggling the bat with a fierce energy, but he was clearly a bit too eager as he swung wildly at the first pitch that bounced in the dirt in front of home plate.

His teammates chattered their advice and encouragement. "Wait 'im out, Terry. Make 'im throw strikes."

Our team countered with equal intensity, "Easy out, easy out … Send 'im home. He's done."

Terry stepped back and took a deep breath. He readied himself, steadied his stance, slowed his warm-up swings to a deliberate pace to channel his energy. The second pitch flew by him, a hard fastball.

"Steerrike two!"

Terry looked down to third base where Paul stood in the coach's box. He seemed to be looking for advice from Paul; none came. He resumed his stance in the batter's box and braced for the next pitch, another fastball.

Crrraaack! came the sound of wood on ball, and his team erupted in cheers and then went silent as the ball drifted into foul territory along the first baseline. But the chatter, the energy, was back, and Terry seemed to be buoyed by the small victory of making contact with a Billy Cline fastball.

"Hey, hey, hey, Terry … You can hit this guy … Pick out a good one. Wait for your pitch, and let it rip!"

Excitement renewed, Terry tapped the plate with his bat, took one and only one warm-up swing, and then crouched low to await the pitch. Billy offered up a slow, looping curveball that for just a moment seemed to hover and stop in the strike zone and then darted down and away. Terry gave a valiant cut at the ball but missed and spun around helplessly.

"Steeerrriiiike three, the … batter … is … out!" announced Ruggles in a sort of mock explanation that needed no embellishment. Terry walked with his head high back to the bench. The scorekeepers on both sides marked a *K* in the proper column.

Druey fired the ball down to third, Mills sent it on to me at second. I threw it sharply to Tommy at short, and he gave it up to Jerry at first. Jerry returned it to Billy in a lazy, cocky flip as our confidence grew with the sound of our chatter.

We were now back to the top of their batting order and Roger Smith. A team does not want to end the inning with their leadoff hitter. His job is to get on base for others to drive him in. But now with two out a sustained rally was not likely, so the other team fell silent as Billy stood confident on the mound, ready to deal the cards.

Roger Smith, excellent athlete, determined competitor, had no room for pessimism or giving up. He scratched the ground inside the batter's box with his left foot but without other show of emotion or rituals. Before the next pitch Dad called time-out from the bench and ran quickly to the third baseline. He lifted both hands and motioned for the outfielders to move back, to a deeper position than where they were playing. Ted in left field, Louie in center, and Tommy Parham in right moved a few steps back and then a few more as Dad continued to wave them back. Tommy found himself standing on the edge of the embankment. Louie was not far from it.

Billy started with another one of his roundhouse curves, but Roger guessed right. He caught the ball with the fat part of the bat and sent it screaming into left center field. Even though Louie was playing deeper than usual, he broke into a dead run as the ball climbed in the sky above his head.

Catching a fly ball is part natural talent, part learning. In a full-out run, the fielder must travel at a speed and on a trajectory so that the ball seems to stay at the same spot in the air. As the ball falls to earth, the fielder then must adjust to keep the ball fixed there until he is directly under it. Louie had natural talent to spare and good enough coaching to know all that. He lifted his gloved hand above his head and slowed his run to just the right speed. He never broke stride as the ball smacked into his outstretched glove and he continued in a wide looping arc back to the infield where he dropped the ball unceremoniously behind the pitcher's mound, as if to say, "No problem. Piece of cake. I do this every day."

Back home we would soon learn Grandmother had a cancer growing in her abdomen. The conflict and distance between my parents was not far away. Russia now had the bomb. Sputnik would follow, and my country would put a nuclear reactor on a boat and send it under the north polar ice cap.

But on this day on the odd-shaped baseball field in Hildebran, the official scorer marked F-8 for the final out of the top of the third inning. I ran in from my position on this warm, clear, blue-sky day. God did indeed seem to be in his heaven.

Except I still had to go back up to bat.

CHAPTER 10

Control

August 19th, 1945

Dear Wife,

I got two little old pretty big nice letters from my pretty big little old family to answer tonight, and I'm pretty glad I have got them too, I am. They were written on the 12th and 14th of this month, but I got them both the same time. Better late than never though, I guess.

Yes, Honey, the alligator hide stuff is pretty expensive, however, it would be worth the price okay except for the ladies purses. I just think that that is too much to pay for a purse, as ladies don't like to carry the same purse a very long time anyway. Those dern things cost close to twenty dollars. If I can find one which does not cost so much though, I will get one for you. Do you need one honey: If you do, I will make it my business to find one for you, and if I can't find one priced less, I will get one of those. After all I would spend the money anyway, and I am pretty sure that I can get one for less, so if you need one don't hesitate to tell me. I would get you some shoes if I knew they would fit: when you get the ones I sent you maybe you can tell me more about how to get a pair that will fit.

As for old Chip, I guess I won't even try to get anything for him, I can't get anything that he needs, as you say he is too little for toys and as for souvenirs, or anything else, he wouldn't know what they were and is too little to appreciate such things also, so I will just wait until I get home to him, then I will get him some things, and do something for him. Maybe it will not be too long now until I come home to my wife and little Chip.

I will bet he will be a heck of a lot like his uncle Edgar. Edgar was a good baby, in fact he was a heck of a good baby, he never cried except when somebody was beating on him and kicking him around. Edgar was the most mistreated baby in the world, nobody had any patience with him. When he would do something that he shouldn't do, nobody tried to correct him, they would just lose their temper and beat the hell out of him, and kick him around, and he would cry and look so pitiful: he never knew what they were doing it for, nobody cared enough about him to try to explain, they just got mad at him. It haunts me now sometimes to think about some of the times I have seen him looking so pitiful and helpless because someone had been beating on him, and he would be trying to figure out why they had done it. To top it off he would forgive so easy, as soon as anyone showed that they were not mad any longer regardless of how long it had been since they had been beating on him he would be laughing and playing with them as much as anybody else. I treated him bad myself, and I can remember how he looked just as plain as if it had been today. If he had not been sent to the orphanage at the time he was, he would have turned out to be the worst outlaw there has ever been, or either a miserable coward, afraid of everybody and everything. I think my little Chip is going to be a whole lot like him, but Mills is sure not going to be treated like he was. You can bet your life on that because it will be over my dead body if he is.

Honey, if you are nervous because you are having such a hard life, when I get home we will change that. Me and Chip, we will change that for you, we will. We will decide where we are going to live and all that when I get home. I don't want you to have to leave your mother and father alone honey, and I am not going to ask you to; I am not even going to ask you to move into another house, even though we could build one next door, but on the other hand there is lots of reasons why we should. You know what they are; but we can thrash those things out alright when I get home, can't we?

Love,
Charlie

THE STORY ABOUT MY uncle Edgar, the youngest of the six siblings in Dad's family, is the only real information I have about my father's life in his parents' home. He told many stories about the orphanage but nothing that came before. Alcohol was almost certainly part of the mix; several family members were touched by the alcohol gene, and Dad once said that his parents died of a vitamin deficiency, beriberi. This seems plausible if one were getting all calories from ethyl alcohol. Given my ultimate profession of psychiatry, I am somewhat embarrassed that I never tried to learn more about this history.

Untold family stories and unanswered family questions notwithstanding, the most compelling part to me about his August 19 letter was his resolve that things be different in the family he would create. For the most part things were different, but around the time of this game, with two parents working hard to care for five children and a dying grandparent, there was real stress and conflict in the family.

One time when harsh words were flying between several of us, my brother issued a pointed challenge to my father's authority. I watched in fear as Dad ran across the yard, his fist drawn back aggressively. My brother lowered his head and raised his hand to shield his face from the blow that was clearly coming. But just before Dad struck, he lowered his hand, and they both stood there looking at each other. It seemed to me that neither knew what to do next. They walked away back to the house. I ran to the barn.

Dad did not always stay his hand. I remember another time when some of us, including my one-year-younger sister, were having our version of a bad day, talking loudly in the house when Dad was sleeping in another room. Awakened by our noise, he charged from his bedroom, belt in hand, and grabbed my sister by the arm and pulled her into another room. I heard the sound of his belt lashes from where I sat stunned and silent. I went into the room to try to comfort her when he returned to the bedroom. I've blocked out more details of that event, but I remember being left with a feeling that things were out of control. Why did he select her? Perhaps it was her voice he heard above the rest of us, but his choice seemed random.

Last of the third inning. My turn back up to bat. I walked to the plate with no expectations of success and as yet no developed rituals like the older boys to gird myself for battle. I shuffled around in the batter's box and looked out at the pitcher, who seemed to sneer at me with contempt and even boredom. "Why even bother with this one?" he said without speaking.

"Strriiiiike one!" came the inevitable call of the first pitch as I watched it scream by me.

"Come on, Drew! Come on, boy!" I heard my teammates rally to support me. "Get that bat off your shoulder! Pick out a good one, and give it a ride!"

I took a few practice swings to get my blood pumping. The next pitch came in low and bounced in front of the plate for ball one. At least I would last more than three pitches. Dad yelled for time-out and called me over for a quick word.

"Listen, the last thing he wants to do is walk you, so he's coming right down the middle of the zone with this next one. Get yourself ready, and take a good cut. It'll be right where you can handle it."

I stepped back in with a sliver of hope and confidence. I cocked the bat and got ready to give it my all. The pitch came in slow and fat, right down the middle of the strike zone. I swung as hard as I could and connected. But instead of hearing that solid smack of bat on ball, I caught it too close to the handle of the bat. This meeting of wood and horsehide produced a weak and hollow twang-like sound and sent the ball softly in the air back to Clayton. He caught it without having to move a step. Worse, he didn't even bother to throw it to the others for the usual tossing around the infield. Why even bother with this one? My humiliation was total, complete.

I turned to the bench to see Dad and some of the others clapping their hands in appreciation and enthusiasm. "That's a start! You made contact!" Other teammates joined in. It felt real. I picked up the pace of my jog back to my seat. So I didn't strike out. It could have been worse.

We were then back to the top of the batting order, Tommy Keller up next, for his second at-bat. Tommy was not only a good athlete, he was a smart one, and he had figured out a pattern to Clayton's pitching. He knew that Clayton liked to get ahead of the hitters and would likely throw a fastball first, usually in the middle of the strike zone. Tommy guessed right and hit the ball squarely. The ball sailed between the third baseman and the shortstop for a solid single to left field.

"Attaboy, Tommy!" came the chorus of cheers from our bench. "Little rally now … Little rally goin' on!" We were on our feet, hands clapping, pumping our fists in the air.

Mills was up next, and by now they respected him, after his base hit the first time up. Dad could have gone the traditional route and used the sacrifice bunt again, but there was already one out. He let Mills swing away. The first pitch screamed in high and close to his head, sending Mills reeling backward, falling to the ground to get out of the way. His face flushed red with anger as he jumped to his feet and brushed the dirt off his pants.

Clayton's next pitch, a slow, sweeping curveball, dropped far outside of the strike zone for ball two. Clayton's teammates raised their level of support, smacking fists in gloves, chatter growing louder. "Okay, okay, bear down now. Git this guy. You da Babe … You da Babe …"

Mills looked down the third baseline at Dad, seeking signs, direction, about what to do on the next pitch. With two balls and no strikes, he knew a hitter's pitch was likely, a pitch designed to be in the strike zone. But if you can work that count to three balls and no strikes, you have the pitcher in a hole. Mills looked for the sign to let the next one go by and see just how wild Clayton might be.

Dad gave no obvious sign to take the pitch, leaving it up to Mills to make the call. Clayton paused for an extra moment before his delivery and took a deep breath, readying himself. The look of contempt and boredom he had for me was gone now, replaced with a serious, determined face. He fired the ball.

Smmaaacckkk! Mills caught the ball solidly, sent it on one bounce sharply right at the feet of the third baseman. Herb saw it coming but had little time to react and get his glove in front of it. Going to his knees, he was able to block it with his chest, and it bounced high in the air. By the time it floated softly back to the ground to his left, Mills was safe at first, and Tommy had slid into second base.

"Way to goooooo! Yes! Smokin'!" Our collective cry rang out as we leaped to our feet. Dad motioned for us to get back to the bench and sit back down, but he was clearly excited too. Two runners on. Only one out.

It was Louie Page's turn at bat. His last time up he had sacrificed, laying down a perfect bunt, so Dad knew he could do it. It was now a question of giving up a second out with another sacrifice or rolling the dice and letting him hit, trying for a big inning rather than a single run or two. No sign came from Dad. Louie was free to go for it.

Louie connected on the first pitch and sent a sharp ground ball down the first baseline. Punk Raby fielded it cleanly but decided on the safe play and ran to tag first base for the sure out number two, rather than throwing it to second for the double play. We now had runners on second and third and our best hitter, Billy Cline, coming to bat.

Clayton called the infielders in for a conference at the pitcher's mound. First base was not occupied, so they could walk Billy. The conference went on longer than pleased Umpire Ruggles. He approached the six players huddled in conversation.

"Let's get this over with," he said calmly but with authority. "Batter's up. Men take your positions and play ball!"

Because of what Billy had done last time up, hitting the ill-fated fly ball over the embankment, there was no chance Clayton was going to pitch to him with two runners in scoring position. Four looping tosses far outside the strike zone put Billy on first. Bases loaded. Two out. Druey Lambert the next hitter.

It was clear this was a key moment in the game. One of our two legitimate stars now had a chance to break the game open. With the way Billy was dominating the game with his pitching, one or two runs could mean the game. A single anywhere in the outfield would easily score Tommy from third and Mills from second base. An extra base hit could clear the bases with the way Billy could run.

Druey did not wait long. He knew that Clayton would not walk him. He took the first expected fastball for a called strike. Then he zeroed in on what he guessed would be a curveball next. Bat hit ball, and he sent the ball soaring over the shortstop's outreached glove. The ball flew toward the gap between the fielders in center and left field.

Tommy broke with the sound of the bat and was halfway home before the ball hit the ground. Mills raced toward third. Dad shed his cap and clipboard and waved his right arm like a windmill, signaling for Mills to keep running, head for home.

Paul in center field did not hesitate. He raced to where the ball would land. He knew that if it got by him, it would roll forever and all four runs would score. At the spot where ball hit ground, he lunged and snared the ball on a short first bounce. With a short hop, Paul regained his balance, planted his right foot, then pivoted back to his left, and in one powerful and graceful motion sent the ball rocketing toward home plate.

When an outfielder tries to throw a runner out at home plate, both accuracy and speed are important. To ensure better accuracy, but with a compromise to speed, the outfielder usually tries to bounce the ball on one hop to the catcher. An attempt to throw it all the way home in the air will most likely see the ball sail off the mark.

But Paul knew he had little time. His throw sped all the way, in the air, to Elliot standing at home plate. The ball sailed true. Elliot caught it, without having to move, with Mills still three strides from home. I saw the surprise on his face, his eyes wide and wild, when he realized Elliot had the ball waiting for him. Crouched in front of the plate to give the tag for the last out of the inning, Elliot quickly took another half step down the line to more completely block the base path.

When a runner is caught this way, he has three options. He can stop and accept the inevitable, try a hook slide and somehow get around the catcher (an unlikely outcome), or blast into the defender and try to dislodge the ball from the mitt. The third option is not illegal. Sometimes it works. It doesn't make you any friends.

Mills chose option three. He lowered his head and with his right shoulder slammed directly into Elliot's chest. Both players careened away from the point of impact, stirring up clouds of dust as they rolled over and over, Mills toward the field of play, Elliot halfway to the backstop.

Everyone on the field that day grew silent as they watched the trajectory of the ball thrown from deep left field, their mouths agape with that I-don't-believe-what-I-just-saw look on their faces. The silence continued as they watched the dust slowly clear from the collision at home plate.

"The runner … is … out!" bellowed Ruggles as he stood, legs wide apart and astride home plate, his right hand clutching his face protector held high above his head to give emphasis and clarity to the call. His gaze turned pointedly toward Elliot, who cradled the ball safely in his catcher's mitt. Ruggles's pose reminded me of a picture of a Roman soldier I saw in a *World Book Encyclopedia*, his sword held high in triumph over a fallen enemy.

Elliot and Mills rose quickly to their feet and stepped toward each other. They stood tall and defiant and stared without speaking. The benches of both teams ran forward to support their respective teammates. Ruggles, who had turned away, looked back and saw the confrontation, and he lunged forward to get between them. Dad was already there a step away, but before anyone spoke, Mills extended his right hand. "Nice play." Elliot accepted, and they shook hands.

Half of the game was now in the books. We led by one to nothing.

A few years ago, I was telling a friend and fellow psychiatrist named David about my childhood baseball idol, Gil Hodges. I described a newspaper article about a time the Dodgers and some other team were in the middle of a brawl and Gil Hodges stepped in as the peacemaker.

The article gave a vivid account of Hodges coming up behind two scuffling players and grabbing first one and then the other with his powerful hands and lifting them off the ground and setting them down on opposite sides of the base path.

My friend replied, "That sounds like a screen memory to me."

A screen memory in psychological terms is a memory that serves as a displacement, a "screen," for a more personal, more meaningful one, perhaps with hidden and painful thoughts and feelings.

Beyond the symbolic, baseball is not life. Life is hard. Baseball is a game. But it is a game that has guided and comforted me. At that time in my life I needed strong men who knew how to be in control. I needed the umpire to understand and enforce the rules, to stand tall and make the call in a way that was unquestioned. My ten-year-old life was not that hard compared to others but hard enough in some important ways. But on that day, on that baseball field, things were not out of control, and the random nature of the way things sometimes happen was suspended for long enough.

CHAPTER 11

Taking Hold

August 21, 1945

Dear Charlotte,

Me too honey, I would like to know when I am coming home to you and Chip. I wish it were immediately if not sooner. But although I don't know when, it is a great comfort to know the war is over and I will be coming home.

Gee honey, all I do now is think about what I am going to do when I get home. I wish I owned a farm and knew something about farming. I don't guess your Mother and Dad would even consider selling their place to us, and I guess I couldn't expect them to, but if we owned it, I could take the $2000 loan from the government and really fix it up good. I would like to come home and take over all the work around there and all the responsibilities. I believe I could do it and work in the bakery too. However it is rather big for my experience, but if I could do what I wanted to with the whole works—I could get along alright—we could live on my income from the bakery and gradually shape the place up to where we wanted it. If I did not have a free hand though, I could not see what should be done and when, and your Dad might resent me and work against me. He might try to outdo me and take advantage of my not knowing what should be done and when, which would give me an inferiority, and make me afraid to take hold of things. And then he might get other people saying I was not worth a damn, and just a dead beat living off of him. I can very plainly remember when I first *came out of the orphanage, and Aunt Dovie was staying with Dorcas and Anna would go to the mill each day, and naturally there would be odds and ends around the house to be done and quite naturally I should do most of them, like cutting grass, etc. Well, Aunt Dovie started jumping the gun and beating me to them. She would mow the lawn, and undertake hard jobs which I didn't notice should have been done, or at least didn't think there was any hurry about, which really there wasn't, and she would work around the house all day long to beat heck just so she could complain to Dorcas when Dorcas came home, and say I would not do it. Well, Dorcas could see what she was doing and that it was unnecessary, and knew she was just doing it against me, but she also tried to impress the neighbors and other people that she was killing herself and I would not help her. Well, the more she tried it the more I let her go, I didn't even attempt to take a hold of things—in fact I drifted further away from them.*

I don't know what chance there is of me running into the same thing with your Dad, but if I would it would make me a very unhappy fellow, and I wouldn't feel like I was the Daddy of a Chip and was doing something for them.

The chance of running into that conflict with your Dad and the envy of the other brothers and sisters of yours for living there, is what makes me afraid to live there.

What we really should do honey, is build a little place across the road there and me start out with just a garden farm and a very little livestock, and gradually turn it into a farm. Then we would be free, independent and safe from gossipers. But I know it would be hard for your Mother and Dad if you were not there in the same house with them, so I am not going to force you to move out from them. However honey, that is our first problem to be solved.

I would like to work in the bakery and start a farm at the same time— honest! And I would have plenty of time for it too working in the bakery. If the hours would run like they did before I came into the army, on Mondays I would get through work about 1:30 or 2:00 o'clock. Tuesdays 3:30, Wednesdays 2:30 Thursdays 3:30 Fridays before noon, and would be off all day Saturday. I would work until about 1:30 on Sundays but that would not affect my part time farming what-so-ever, and would give me Sunday evenings and nights for whatever we wanted to do on Sundays. The chances are those hours will not be the same but they can't be far off from that, and I know I would still be able to have enough hours at home for part time farming. I am interested in it too honey, I really am. I am a whole lot more settled than even before just coming overseas and I personally don't think I was very bad for being unsettled, although I did like to break monotonous routines and just say the heck with things sometime. I still feel that way to a certain extent, but not enough to hinder the wheels from rolling.

Are you and Chip doing okay honey? Gee I will be glad when I can come home to you.

Love,
Charlie

THE PLAN THAT MY father outlined in his August 21 letter indeed became the basic structure of my parents' life upon his return. He was hired at the bakery with hours that allowed for part-time farming. Chickens for eggs and meat, a one-acre vegetable garden, a cow for fresh milk, and regular litters of pigs for slaughter were the basic mix. Later this schedule allowed for time for coaching baseball games on summer afternoons.

I don't know how he worked out his relationship with his father-in-law, but everyone stayed in the old house, and they worked the existing land. My grandfather died January 31, 1948, a year and eleven days after I was born. So I guess Dad then became the man to "take hold of things" and decide what needed to be done, regardless of any extended-family resentment or gossip.

Some of my earliest memories are of gathering eggs from the laying hens, watching Dad milk the cow, and helping carry table scraps to the pigpen. One vivid memory comes from a cold winter morning. Just up from a night of sleep, I walked into our kitchen to find Dad struggling to build a fire in the kitchen stove. On his head he wore an old army cap, with earflaps hanging down, and he was fumbling to light a match with his hands still in his thick, bulky gloves as he knelt before the firebox.

He was just in from the early morning chores. A bucket of fresh milk on the kitchen table streamed a cloudy vapor that curled to the ceiling. On the floor in front of Dad lay old newspapers and kindling, ready to be lit, but the thickness of his gloves and the shiver from his hands inside them prevented him from successfully starting the fire. As he pulled off the clumsy gloves, he turned to look at me, his face beet red from the cold and his eyebrows frosted with droplets of ice.

"You get back in that bed now … I'll have this fire goin' in a minute." He spoke in a matter-of-fact way as he balled up his fists and warmed them by placing them in his armpits, rolling his shoulders forward to envelop his stiff, cold hands.

I had no real understanding of the context of this moment, of his journey back from the war, to baker-farmer, to becoming the one to get things done. I did appreciate the fact that I could crawl back into the warm bed and know that later that morning a fire in that stove would fry eggs and heat soup. I knew that when night came again, there would be wood and coal fires in several stoves throughout the house. One stove would heat the old solid-piece irons that would be wrapped in bath towels and placed at the foot of our beds to warm our feet and comfort us in sleep during the winter nights ahead.

Top of the fourth inning and we were now in the lead, although our enthusiasm lagged after we scored only one run in our at-bat. Druey Lambert's hit with the bases loaded should have led to bigger things. The spirits on the other side grew because of the play that Paul and Elliot had made for the third out. The game was now exactly half over. It seemed unlikely that one run would be the end of the scoring. Enthusiastic chatter from their bench grew louder as they readied for their turn in the inning.

Jesse Raby stood in for his second attempt at bat. Billy threw him the same high, hard fastball that struck him out the first time. Swing and a miss. Strike one. Jesse moved back out of the batter's box and pounded the ground with his bat in slow-motion, controlled frustration. Perhaps this helped steady him as he took the next two pitches, both high and out of the strike zone.

At that point Druey, behind the plate, sensed our energy lag, and he chastised the infielders. "Hey! Where's the chatter? Let's get it goin' now. Are we dead?" He pointed in turn at each of the infielders, giving a nod of his head to each, calling us back to action.

We responded, "Hey, Billy, Billy, you the man! Fire it in there!"

"Hey now ... Hey now! Blow it by him!" came our collective cry.

Billy tugged on his cap, pounded the ball into his glove. Spit. Looked in for the sign from Druey. He shook his head twice, refusing the first two offerings by his catcher. He wanted to throw the fastball. It came in too low, and Jesse held back again.

"Ball three!" barked Ruggles.

Billy regrouped and again waved off the catcher's sign. A fastball right down the middle of the zone got the call.

"Steeerrrriikkke two!"

Full count to their leadoff hitter in the top of the fourth. A pitcher never wants to let the first batter of the inning get on base. Lots of big rallies start that way. But the next pitch drifted outside, and Jesse let it go by.

"Ball four. Batter, take your base," instructed Ruggles with a clarity that seemed unneeded.

Next up was Herb Livertt, who wasted no time. He slapped the first pitch down the first baseline on the ground. Jerry scooped it up and fired a perfect toss to Tommy covering second. He caught it cleanly and set himself for the throw to first base to complete the double play.

What happened next illustrates the mistaken notion that baseball is a no-contact sport. As Tommy drew back his arm for the throw, Jesse made a rolling slide directly into him, cutting his legs out from under him. Tommy fell headfirst over Jesse, and the ball somehow flew straight up in the air above them. Billy moved in instantly to retrieve the ball and keep Herb from advancing.

Coming so soon after the collision at home between Mills and Elliot, it might have looked to some like retribution, but no one reacted with anger. This was just good, clean, hard-nosed baseball. Tommy dusted himself off and trotted back to his position. Jesse did the same and ran back to his bench to take the pats on the back for a good play. It kept the rally alive. One on, one out. We still had a one-run lead, but now Paul Fowler was up for his next turn.

It might have been better if Herb had reached second base. Then first would be open and would justify walking Paul intentionally, but with one out and a runner on first, a free pass to the batter just isn't the right play.

Paul stepped up to the plate and completed his series of hitches, dips, and taps. Billy's first pitch slid inside for a ball. His second pitch was called a strike. Their bench howled in disagreement, but Paul never changed his expression. He was determination personified. He had watched that last pitch all the way into the catcher's mitt as if he were gathering information for the next one.

Whatever he learned he put to good use and connected solidly on Billy's slow curve. The ball flew just out of reach over the shortstop's head and sent Louie again in full stride in center field to chase it down. This time his outstretched glove touched the ball only enough to slow it down, and the ball bounced away. Herb raced around second base and headed toward third. Paul took a big turn around first and dug for second. Their bench erupted in cheers, urging the runners on. By the time Louie caught up to the ball and fired it back to the infield, Herb had crossed the plate, and Paul had slid safely into third for a triple. Tie game. One to one. Still just one out.

Dad called time-out and called all the infielders to the mound. "Okay, no real damage done here. Keep your heads, and we'll be fine. We got past Paul, and he didn't hurt us that bad. Billy, stay focused now. You got some people behind you that can catch the ball, so you don't have to do it all yourself."

He looked right at Billy and then at Druey. Each nodded their reply.

Up next was Clayton Lowman, a good hitter. Dad decided against walking him intentionally to create a force play at second and a chance to end the inning with a double play. Billy pitched to him carefully but still ended up walking him after running the count to three balls and one strike.

Elliot came next in the batting order. A lot of their guys were swinging at the first pitch as if they had figured out what Billy liked to throw first. Elliot did the same but hit only a soft ground ball down the first baseline. Jerry fielded it while moving a step toward home and fired it to Druey to catch the runner coming in from third. But Paul was smarter than that. He anticipated the play and held his ground. By the time the ball reached the catcher, Elliot had sprinted safely to first. Still only one run in, but now the bases were loaded. Norman Bess up to bat.

Dad started to call another time-out for another trip to the mound, but Billy held up his hand to stop him. "We got it." He nodded confidently. I think Billy understood that he had made it through the really good hitters in the lineup with "no real damage done." He now faced the hitters that came last in the batting order. He knew things would get easier. He walked quickly back to take his position. He looked confident. We sensed it. The chatter returned.

"Hum, Babe … Hum, Babe … Come, Babe … Come, Babe!"

"Here we go … Here we go! Got him lookin' … Throw some smoke now!"

Billy's first pitch was not the hard fastball but a slow, looping curve that caught Norman off balance. He swung and caught it weakly on the end of his bat, rolling it slowly back to the mound. Billy fielded it cleanly, but he was not confident that he had time for the second to first double play. He tossed it softly to Druey at home to force Paul out at home. Norman took first, bases still loaded, but at least Paul was out of the picture. Two outs.

Billy again stood confidently on the mound, staring down the next batter. Mickey Lynn was up again, the right fielder who had run down the bank and supposedly caught Billy's blast. Billy squinted his eyes as if to say, "I remember you."

It would be wrong to say that this bit of special attention rattled Mickey, but it did seem to get into his head in some way. Mickey stepped out of the box and looked down at the ground, hesitating before taking his place. Maybe he was simply aware of the situation, that a hit here would do some serious damage, and he felt the pressure to deliver. A missed opportunity here would mirror the last half inning and swing the momentum back to us.

Billy came with the fastball. "Steeerrrriiiiike one!" Mickey knew it was a good pitch and that he could not have done anything with it. He gave a little hop up and down, with the bat on his shoulder, without leaving the batter's box. I thought he looked spooked.

Billy fired again. "Steeerrriiiike two." This time Mickey stepped back out of the box, and his expression changed to an angry snarl, as if to try to pump up his own energy and confidence. But by the time he gave a hard, valiant swing at the third pitch, the ball was already by him and resting safely in the catcher's mitt.

"Steeerrriiiike three. The batter's out!" Ruggles echoed the obvious.

Billy walked deliberately from the mound. No jumping up and down celebrating. A steady walk. Not too slow, not too fast. No glaring, staring, gloating, or any real acknowledgement of the moment. Routine stuff. It was as if he was saying, "Nothing special here. It's what I do." It's the kind of thing that people do when they are ready to take hold of things.

CHAPTER 12

Anticipation

August 25th, 1945

Dear Charlotte,

Gee honey haven't you been getting my letters? I have been writing every other day—just like clockwork, but yours have been kind of slow too, so I think they just slowed up delivery somewhere along the line to celebrate victory over Japan. I wish it had been me sending that cablegram telling you I was coming home. I don't even know yet how long to expect to have to stay in the army. We were told that they would start letting men out as fast as they could, and the first benefactor would be age, all over 38 first, then points, 75 and over first. I did not have but 52 when they counted them up, and if they would count them now up to date, I still would not have but 72 counting Chip. I told them I had a Chip at home, but I will keep the certificate for a while just in case things get snafued and I have to prove again that I have got a Chip. The way things look right now it will be around to the spring of the year before I will be getting out. That would not be too bad if only I knew when, so I could count on it, and if I could get home a time to see you and Chip. How is your mother getting along honey, I hope she is okay by this time. How is my Chip coming? Is he still propped up between those two pillows? Well if he wants to ride the bull, and if the bull don't mind, I don't see why I should object.

I'm sorry the shoes didn't fit, if you will send me the inner soles of an old pair, and draw an outline of the whole shoe, I can have some made. I don't know how long I will be here, but it looks like they are going to leave me here as a permanent part man to maintain this base for while—they have assigned me to a permanent job running the projectors for the movie here. Those shoes didn't cost but $5. You can sell them or give them to someone, or do whatever you want to with them.

Blanch wrote that Andrew was in the hospital with pneumonia. It hit him just like it did me last summer.

Well now gee honey, that all depends, if I have to stay in the army many more months. I hope you have not bought your last dollars worth of stamps, but what I really hope is that before many months are up, I will be home with you and my little Chip.

Love,
Charlie

THE AUGUST 25 LETTER is one of many over the next few weeks in which Dad talks about the interminable waiting—long days, boring days, despite the sense of relief from the war's end. This may be a time that he first developed a kind of philosophy of life having to do with anticipation. My sister told me a few years ago that he once talked to her about what makes life meaningful for him. The answer for him was to have something to look forward to, something that he could anticipate. He felt that most of the events and experiences of life are disappointments; that whatever one desires, whatever one hopes to achieve or attain will mostly not live up to the promise. The real joy in life is to find the next thing for which to plan. And when the day of that event comes and it is not as rewarding as the build-up, then you move on and find another next thing to look forward to.

I find this point of view a bit sad—and funny—and consistent with the man I knew when we were older. I remember one conversation late in his life about watching the Atlanta Braves play baseball on television. He liked the Braves but said he always hoped the other team would win, although it would make him happy if the Braves did win. This was much better than to hope the Braves would win and then feel bad when they lost.

This way of thinking is some of what baseball is all about. There is only one World Series winner, and everyone else will just have to wait till next year. All the players, except those on the winning team, must hang their heads, put up the gloves and bats for the winter, and wait for springtime. That becomes the thing to look forward to.

Winter will end, and at long last the month of March arrives. It's warm enough for baseball but windy. The true believers pull their hats down tight on their heads and bundle up enough to be outside and toss the ball around, running on brown grass and leftover unraked leaves. Finally April arrives, with daffodils, tulips, and greener grass. Hope is alive. Everything is new. All baseball teams have the same record; no one has lost a game yet. Paul Fowler unplugs his television so his eyes stay sharp. Young men look to themselves to see how much taller and stronger they have grown. Older men make wishes for just one season more.

The mighty Casey's strikeout is still months away. Joy will remain for a time. The air is never cleaner or fresher. Life is filled with … anticipation.

❧

We were now tied at one run each, going into the bottom of the fourth inning. Dad called a short conference with our three batters who were scheduled up first in the inning.

"Let's change things up a little here; let's switch our strategy," he said with a kind of wink, smile, and a twist of his head to indicate we were going to play a little mind game with their pitcher. "I think Clayton is getting a little tired and a little wild, so we're gonna wait him out. Don't take a cut at anything till he gets two strikes on you, and then make sure if you do swing that you swing at a strike."

Ted Icard was up first. He looked at the first pitch as it came in low and inside, bouncing in the dirt and skipping around Elliot all the way to the backstop.

"Atta boy; atta boy! Make him throw strikes!" We weighed in from the bench.

Clayton's next pitch was close. Ruggles closed his fist and turned slightly preparing to lift his right hand for the called strike, but then he thought better of it and spoke just loudly enough for batter and catcher to hear. "Nooooo, not quite … just a little inside. Ball two."

Anyone who could see Elliot's face through his catcher's mask would have seen his look of frustration at the call, but he kept the unwritten rules about not arguing with the umpire. Don't go dramatic. Don't turn around and look the umpire in the face. Don't do anything to show him up or call him out. So Elliot held onto the ball just a few seconds longer than usual before he threw it back to Clayton, a subtle and acceptable way to show disagreement. Clayton caught the ball and turned away, slamming the ball into his glove in obvious frustration.

Ted stepped away from the plate and looked down at Dad for a sign. Dad's brief nod confirmed the strategy, and Ted stood with bat on shoulder and watched ball three bounce in front of the plate. Our bench raised the level of chatter. "Wild as a buck! Wild as a buck! Stick a fork in him; he's done!"

With a count of three balls and no strikes it's almost always an automatic take for the next pitch. Knowing this, most pitchers take their time and get the next pitch over for a strike. But Dad was right: Clayton was tired, and he was getting wild. The fourth pitch sailed outside for ball four. Our first batter stood on first base. No outs.

Elliot called time-out and rose from his catcher's crouch to go to the mound and talk with Clayton. After lots of nodding and some spitting later, Clayton was ready to go. Jerry Rudisill was up next and obeyed orders to wait Clayton out. But the first pitch was right down the middle of the strike zone, and the next one came in slow and fat, a perfect hitter's pitch. I think I could see Jerry straining inside and out to hold back and let it go by. He got strike two for his efforts.

"Swing away now; take some cuts," barked Dad, making sure Jerry knew that with two strikes he was free to swing. Jerry was all too pumped up by now and took a hard swing at a ball that was way outside and way low. He missed by a foot and made the long, slow walk back to the bench. One on, one out.

Dad called the next batter, Tommy Parham, over for more instruction. "Tommy, I still want you to wait him out, but I want you to act like you're not. Look like you're going to swing. Go ahead and swing at the first pitch; then go back into the waitin' until he gives you a second strike."

Tommy understood the game. He stepped up to the plate with a show of enthusiasm, even anger, swinging the bat back and forth with energy and power. The first pitch came in slow, looking as big as a pumpkin, and Tommy connected. But with such a slow offering and Tommy out in front of it, he lined it hard but clearly foul down the first baseline.

"That's what I'm talkin' about!" yelled Dad.

We all chimed in with our own efforts. "Got him goin' … got him goin'! Pick out a good one, and let it rip!"

Tommy then went back to the waiting mode and took the next two pitches outside and low and then had to scramble out of the way of another that came inside and just missed hitting him. He got back in the batter's box quickly, whipping the bat back and forth, ready for battle, aware that his opponent knew this was the pitch to hit, three balls and one strike, clearly in favor of the batter.

Clayton stood tall on the mound. He did not look like someone who was tired or in a jam. He held a defiant, determined look for a few extra seconds before he threw his next pitch, a fastball that came in knee-high and heading for the outside edge of home plate. Tommy held back. The ball dropped just out of the strike zone for ball four. Two on base. One out. And now it was my turn for my second at-bat.

I remember the next few moments as clearly as any childhood memory with my dad. He wrapped an arm around my shoulder and spoke in a reassuring way. "Okay, let me tell you the same thing I told Tommy. You don't have to swing until you get two strikes. But you do have to act like you are going to swing. Do your best. You've already done some good things in this game, so don't put pressure on yourself. Go up there, and give it your best."

As I walked up to face Clayton, I knew I was not going to hit this guy. But he might walk me or hit me, and if that happened it would be just fine. Mainly I concentrated on what I needed to do to look like I was a hitter. I tried to copy Tommy. Look determined. Take my warm-up swings like I meant them. I hoped that he was as wild as Dad thought, but even if I did strike out, we still had one more out.

Clayton was not fooled by my act. He tossed the first two pitches softly down the middle of the strike zone. I watched them as if I was going to eat them, but I knew who was the prey.

"Swing away now. Swing away," my teammates encouraged me. I did swing away, waving at the still air, generating only the most minimal disruption of the space around the plate as the ball sailed by me into Elliot's mitt.

"Good cut. Good cut," shouted my dad. "You'll get him next time. You'll get him then."

We still had runners on base and Tommy Keller coming up. One last chance to score this inning, to break this game open. But Tommy wasn't sure about whether or not to keep going with the wait-him-out strategy. He ran a few steps toward Dad, who met him and whispered a quick instruction in Tommy's ear behind a cupped hand.

Tommy took his batting position and waved his bat furiously as he looked out at his adversary for the first pitch. Clayton wasted no time, delivering a hard fastball that came in at the knees and directly over the plate.

"Steeeeerriiiike one!" came the call.

Tommy kept his stance without moving, ready again for the next pitch as soon as the first one was by him. He watched a slow, looping curve sail far outside, and our bench woke up from a brief slumber. "Oookaaaay. Oookaaaay! Now you got 'im."

The chatter from the other side grew in response. "Bring it in there, Babe; bring it! Fire it in; he's lookin' for a walk."

It was now the last half of the fourth inning. Score one to one. Two men on. Two men out. The count to the batter was one ball and one strike. We were about as tied up as a game can get. One good swing that connected could change that. Tommy looked ready. Clayton looked ready. The pitch flew toward the waiting batter, another curve. Tommy took it for ball two.

"Hey, hey! Got him in a hole. Throw some dirt over him; he's a goner!" someone chimed in from our bench.

Tommy stood ready again. Clayton pumped and fired a hard fastball.

"Steeeeerriiiiike two!" boomed Ruggles.

No one on our bench still sat. No one in the field of play was silent or dawdled or looked distracted. The fielders pounded their fists into their gloves, gave it their best chatter, poised on the balls of their feet, everyone ready for whatever would come next.

People who think baseball is boring have little sense of the value, of the excitement, of anticipation. In other sports games that have a time clock, there always seems to be some action moving the competition forward, a flow to the game. There is an urgency to getting the ball and moving it toward whatever counts as a score. But in baseball there is no clock, and there are big pauses in the action, the flow. These pauses can add weight to what is to happen next, because they are also opportunities to let down your guard, to become distracted and not be ready. The next pitch, the next hit, the next time at bat could be the one—the one that defines, the one for which you are remembered.

So you must stand ready. If you are in the field, you cannot be distracted. In the outfield the next pitch could come screaming toward you or over your head in a heartbeat. If you are in the infield, you can never let your mind wander. That runner on first base could steal you blind before you get over to cover the base. And when it is your time at bat, you must be ready. In each game you get only two or three, rarely more than four, times at the plate. It can all slip by you. You can miss your opportunity if you do not seize the opportunity.

Clayton rocketed his next pitch and at the same time gave a loud, drawn-out grunt-scream that we had not heard from him before. The ball seemed to travel to home plate fueled by the booming sound of Clayton's voice. The ball flew by Tommy with such speed that he stood motionless with the bat still on his shoulder.

"Steeeerrriiike three!" boomed Ruggles in a spirit echo to Clayton.

CHAPTER 13

Risk

September 12th, 1945

Dear Charlotte,

Hey there honey, I got a couple of letters from you today. Darling, I need you just as much as you do me, and I am just as lonely for you. I want to live with you and Chip. I know I don't have to work as much as you do, and I don't have any obligation, but I am lonely and want to be with you and Chip. I've seen lots of places and things and have had chances to do things that many people would enjoy doing—but I just don't feel like it, and all I want is to come home to you and Chip.

Since I've been in the army I've learned to hate people, especially groups of people. An individual person I can judge him and like him, but when there is a snafu, I just like to get as far away from them as possible. I can't stand a crowd of people any more. Since I've been overseas I have spent most all of my time in solitude. The average stranger I see, I just hate him on sight. I don't know what has made me that way, but thats the way I am and that's why I want to come home so badly and live with my family.

I don't think taking care of your mother is going to be much trouble for us. It is true we won't be as free as we might like to be, but then the chances are we couldn't afford to be that free anyway. I can't think of anything I would want to do which her being there, and even bed stuck, would prevent us from doing. I think one of our most important things to do concerning her, is to watch ourselves and not make her think that she is a burden. For instance when we want to go somewhere, and can by getting someone else to stay with her, we should hardly mention the matter to her, just go, and not go through a lot of asking her if it would be okay for us to get someone to stay with her when we are gone, etc. then she wouldn't think so much about if it were not for her we would be more free, or things like that. In other words, see that she is taken care of, but not letting her know we are obligated to do so. Us just do what we want and act like we want to, simply ignoring her with the matter, but always seeing that someone is with her, or whatever the case may require, without talking to her about it.

Your mother is a mighty good woman, and certainly has never done me any harm, and I really believe she always meant well dealing with you, whether it turned out for the best or not. I think a lot of your mother and am willing to help take care of her. The chances are we won't be able to build a home of our own as long as she is living and the more we mention a home of our own to her the more she will feel she is in the way. The more I think about it the more I feel that I don't want to live there after she is gone, even if she would sell us the place. There would always be your brothers and sisters begrudging us of the place, and if we would always live there we would always feel old, and too much attached to the old place and have old ideas about things. We need to live in a new environment, git something that is a novelty to us or we will be old, very old, before we should be. I think we should move to a new locality, maybe even out of state, make a new set of people for our friends. There is nothing wrong with the people you know around Hildebran, as far as I know, but what we need to do is become acquainted with a new bunch of people together so that both of us will know the same people as friends. I just don't think we can ever be able to mix with either the Valdese or the Hildebran people with both of us at ease and feeling free and friendly among them. If we got acquainted with a new bunch of people together, we would both know them and feel the same way about them. It is hard to become acquainted with new people and sometimes takes a long time, and you feel like you will never know them and like them as much as you did your old friends, but it finally works out, and usually one is glad they made the new friends. I also want to make friends who feel more or less the same way we do about matters, that is, people who we can enjoy being around, and them enjoy being around us, without the old feeling of obligations, and they owe us a visit, or dinner or we owe them a visit or something.

Honey, there is just gobs and gobs of guys going home from here. I think they have all the guys down to 80 points on orders. I have 73 points to date. I had 53 in May when they counted them, and since then they counted them up to date and with Chip I have 73 now, so if they keep sending them home as fast as they have been, I stand a good chance of being home for xmas. But I don't know if they will keep sending them home, they might stop at a certain point, but I hope not. I don't know what they will do about closing the base yet. I want to get home as fast as I can, before xmas if possible.

Honey, I guess old Chip would have the colic if he ate his socks. Gee he must have too much goat about him. What can I get you and him for xmas, honey? I am truly sorry at choosing presents for anyone.

Honey, I hope it isn't too long before I will be home with you and Chip. I want to keep writing until I do get there.

Love,
Charlie

THIS LETTER GAVE ME the opportunity to reflect on many things about my life and my father's life. First, I am surprised to read the words about hating people. I suppose every locale has a share of hateful people, but I never heard him talk about people in this way. I remember his cautions about making assumptions about people who are different from you, and once he admonished me in a gentle but firm way about my teasing a physically less capable classmate. I believe most in his community would have seen him as a friendly, fair-minded, and well-liked person.

I've read a few things about the difficulties of men serving in a peacetime army and how this presents challenges not found during the active time of war. With no common enemy, no higher purpose of service to guide thoughts and behavior, soldiers may value their comrades less during the peace. Perhaps this drove my father's feelings about his time as wasted, needlessly away from home and family. He had less tolerance for snafus.

I can't help but wonder about the alternative life that Dad proposed in the letter—no growing up within walking distance of eight pairs of uncles and aunts and close to a score of cousins. How would I have changed without the experience of going to school with the same peers from first grade through high school?

Realistically speaking, there was never a real chance our family would leave for another state, at least not after Grandmother managed to live a dozen years postwar, allowing my parents and siblings to settle into life in Hildebran. Mother was born and died on that small farm. Fully a part of the people with whom she shared time and community, she drew my father into it. For her there was no alternate life. And almost as important, there might never have been the second-greatest baseball game ever played.

Top of the fifth inning, score tied one to one. The youngest of the other team's pair of brothers, Terry Smith, came to bat first in their half of the inning. I have a clear and dramatic childhood memory of Terry leaping headfirst from the wing wall of the Henry River Dam into the water. I marveled at the magnificent and graceful arch of his twenty-foot plunge into the river that powered the small hosiery mill in Henry River Mill Village. We played there around the dam and reservoir that generated electricity for the mill, a dozen or so boys in a game of tag, the kind of sport we all knew before organized games were available in the community.

Terry was fearless. He was never tagged "it" as we ran along the old bridge that crossed the river, sometimes scaling the walls and roof of the mill itself. The numerous nooks and crannies of the walls, doors, and windows of the factory served well as hiding places. But if Terry was cornered, he had the ultimate escape. Like a cat he could shimmy up the concrete supports of the dam, run the short distance along the stairs to the wing wall, sprint along the three-foot-wide walking area that had no railing on either side and then launch himself—no holding back, no fear, full trust in his ability to find the right landing in the water. *Can't catch me!*

This game of tag was like the game at the orphanage where boys would jump the locomotive moving through the grounds and see who had the courage to stay on the longest. This was the kind of game that Dad feared for us to play, so he gave us baseball.

"Batter up!"

The sun's heat had eased slightly with the passing of the day. It was now close to four o'clock in what was still one of the longest days of sunlight of the year. Some of the fielders shielded their eyes, battling the sun now lower in the sky.

As fearless at the plate as he was in the water, Terry crouched low in his batting stance and crowded close to home plate, making it just a bit harder for Billy to find the strike zone. Ruggles called the first two pitches as balls.

Billy took a little speed off his next fastball to make sure it found the right spot, and Terry caught just enough of it to send a soft pop-up fly ball into short right-center field. Whether it was the sun or simply indecision about who was to take charge of the play, the two closest outfielders each looked to the other to make the catch. The ball fell untouched to the ground for a single. Not only was their leadoff hitter on base, but he was the number nine batter, so they were now back to the top of the order with their best batsmen coming up. Roger Smith took his place to face Billy.

The other side's chatter rang out. "Got a little rally goin' now … Hey … hey!"

"Okay, Roger … Roger, tee off on this guy now … Let's get around the bases now!"

If Billy was discouraged, he didn't show it. He had to face the top of the lineup eventually. He leaned forward, looking in to take the sign from Druey. Billy's first pitch blew by Roger's healthy cut for strike one.

To everyone's surprise, including his own teammates, Terry broke for second base on the pitch. No one expected their youngest player to be stealing a base. From the sound of the gasps from his teammates it seemed obvious that no one had given him the steal sign. But it was such a surprise that neither I nor the shortstop got over to take a throw. Druey held back and made no offer to try to throw him out. Despite the lack of a throw, Terry lunged in a headfirst slide into second. His arms wrapped around the base, he looked up, apparently amazed to see himself alone and no one near him with the ball.

His teammates' chatter changed from gasps to cheers. "Waaaayyyy to goooooo!"

"Smokin' … smokin'! Here we go now; got 'em goin'!"

Druey called time-out and walked slowly to the mound, calling all the infielders to join him. Dad nodded and stayed on the bench, letting the players work it out. Nothing complicated came from Billy or Druey, just a "Let's get our heads up now."

The question now was whether Terry would try to steal third base. Many good base runners say it is easier to steal third rather than go from first to second. The pitcher can't see the runner on second without turning his head all the way around, so keeping up with the runner can distract him from what he's trying to do with the batter. Billy waved for me to move a little closer to second base to make Terry think Billy might try to pick him off. Terry shortened his lead from the base. Billy fired strike two. Terry stayed put.

Before the next pitch, Terry took a longer lead off second base. I played a little cat-and-mouse with him, feigning a move toward the base and then moving quickly back to my fielding position. Roger took a high pitch for ball one. Terry danced and faked and threatened to run but again held back.

Billy readied for the next pitch. Terry took a longer lead. And this time when I moved toward the base, I saw Billy whirl around and set himself to fire the ball to me. This caught Terry by surprise, and the ball got to me with Terry still two steps from the bag. Unfortunately, Billy bounced it in the dirt in front of me, and the best I could do was block it with my chest and keep it from going into center field. The ball rolled a few feet away, and Terry slid back in safely.

By then Terry's teammates were fed up with his risk taking. Paul walked to the baseline and bellowed, "That's enough. Stay there. Let us drive you in!"

Roger took two more balls while Terry stayed close to the base. Then he hit a high pop-up in the infield that Tommy at shortstop handled cleanly. One out. Next, Punk Raby stepped in for his third at-bat. Druey remembered how Billy handled him in the first inning and called for three high, hard fastballs that sent him back to the bench. Out number two. Next up was Herb Livertt, and if he kept the inning alive, Paul was again due up.

I'm not sure how he would have said it in words, but Terry obviously concluded that the plan for him to wait and let his teammates drive him in was not working. On the first pitch Terry broke for third. Druey caught the ball cleanly and sent it crisply down to Mills at third. The throw sailed high over his head and into left field.

Terry bounced up from his slide and raced toward home. His team reacted as one, jumping up from their seats, cheering him home with what would be the go-ahead run. But our left fielder, Ted, saw how everything was developing and moved to just the right spot to back up the play. He caught the errant throw on one bounce and sent it whistling back in toward home plate. In that fraction of a second, when we all saw the ball and the runner arriving at virtually the same time, all sound stopped; all breathing stopped, save for the players involved, one running for the score, the other reaching out for the ball.

Terry once again shot himself headfirst, a human cannonball, toward the safety of home base, but Druey had the ball waiting for him. The ball set firmly in his mitt, Druey applied the tag solidly to Terry's shoulder and then stepped gracefully to the side as Terry tumbled past him, reaching out with both arms for the plate.

"The runner is out!" cried Ruggles.

The cheers returned to our side, and the other team stood in total silence. Just like everyone else on my team I jumped up and down, joining the celebration of hugs and pats on the back. But I also couldn't help but take note of the contrast between the moment just before and the one just after Terry was tagged out. None of his teammates helped him up off the ground. They turned and walked silently back to the bench. They left him to pick himself up. Had he been safe, he would have ridden the shoulders of his comrades-in-arms as a hero. But now he had made the last out when their best two hitters were set to bring him in.

$\sim$

The analogy between war and sports permeates our language, a shared common terminology. I think this is disrespectful to those who have been in war. Sports is a game, an elective proposition. Yet I can't help but wonder about my Dad's attitude toward his fellow soldiers and the behaviors he noted that led him to feel hatred. Was that anything like the snafu of Terry's third out? Does our connectedness ride so much on such events?

Just for the record, I had nothing but respect and admiration for Terry and his attempts to make something happen. No holding back. No fear. Launch yourself into the game, into life. Go for it, Terry. We should all be so free.

CHAPTER 14

End in Sight

September 22, 1945

Dear Charlotte,

General George C. Marshall, army chief of staff told congress today that the army point system will be abolished entirely by late winter and in the meantime it plans reduction of points required for discharge to seventy on October first and sixty on November first. That was a bulletin that we got a couple of days ago, and it sure sounds good to me. That would mean I will be home next month honey. It seems too good to be true, but gosh, how I am hoping it is true. Gee honey, October is just a little more than a week off, can that be true, or will there be an obstacle blocking it in my case somewhere. I hope not.

That builds my hopes up tremendously, although it seems too good to be true that I will get out next month, I know I will get out sooner than I expected. I really didn't expect to get out before next spring, but if they are even just talking about doing things that fast I will get out before then. I should be out by Christmas anyway, or at least in the States by Christmas surely to heck.

How are you and my Chip honey? Does Chip know his daddy has a good chance of being home pretty soon now? Although it can be sooner than I expected, it can't be too soon to make me happy. Tomorrow would not be too soon to suit me. I want to get home to my wife and see what my little Chip is like. I have a good idea what he is like, but I want to see him in flesh and blood and stuff.

I will have to come home and take care of my family, a wife, a Chip, and myself, but that is what I want to do. I can take care of myself better with my wife and Chip with me. We will get along somehow honey. I don't know just what we will do to get along, but we will. I will go out and get the bacon and somehow and while I am not out getting bacon you, me and Chip are going to enjoy life together. It is going to be enjoyable for me just taking care of you and Chip.

Is your mother getting along okay? How about her doctor and hospital bill, who is taking care of that? I hope she is resting good and everything. The rest that she will have to get while she is laid up in bed might do her good in a way. If it does not bother her in her mind too much, the rest should be good for her. That is if she does not have to suffer too much. Did she get the letter I wrote her?

Honey, I am going to be hoping like the dickens that all men with seventy points get out of the army by October, but I guess all that I can do about it is wait and see and hope in the meantime. Would you like for me to come home next month sometime? I have seventy three points and I don't see any reason why I would not get out if they bring the points down that low, but it is hard to realize that I will be home soon, and things can happen so it won't be true, but I can hope and I will hope.

Goodnight darling and sweet dreams.

Love,
Charlie

THE LAST HANDFUL OF letters are pretty much all the same. Other than his eagerness and hopefulness, it seems he had run out of much to say. The waiting—it was all about the waiting. So I study the letters, trying to read between the lines, and I note that the last fifteen or so were typed, not handwritten. I also see better grammar and spelling and more distinct and appropriate paragraphs. Perhaps he used this time to teach himself typing and other things about composition.

I wonder if those typed letters had anything to do with the fact my parents made me take typing when I was a sophomore in high school. I remember protesting, asking, "Why in the world would I need to learn to type? I'm not going to be somebody's secretary." But my parents made me take typing, and forty years later my daughter dragged me into the computer age. That has a real symmetry; even though my daughter did not take typing, she learned keyboarding.

∞

Like my father's time in the military, this baseball game was winding down. Now in the bottom of the fifth, the next-to-the-last inning at this age level, score tied. We all knew something could happen to end this game quickly.

My brother came to bat first in the inning. He had two hits already, and I think he had earned a real respect from Clayton and the others at this point. But there was little chatter from their infield and less from our bench. The collective energy of all the players seemed spent. It was as if we just all wanted to know what was going to happen, beginning with what Mills was going to do.

Mills did not have a lot of rituals at the plate. He stood in calmly, taking warm-up cuts that were more of a formality than a show of aggression or something to pump his spirit. The first pitch trailed outside for ball one. The next one came in slow and fat, and Mills connected but pulled it foul to even the count. Roger ran in from short for a quick conversation with Clayton. I don't know what they said, but I recall a sense of pride that my brother would be the object of special strategy from these older boys.

This game was one of the first times I got any sense about what it was like to be on a team. I felt both power and comfort that I was in the game with my big brother, my dad, and players as talented and strong as Billy Cline and Paul Fowler. I sat on the bench feeling a kind of energy, a glow, watching it unfold, teammates sitting on my right and left side. Amazingly, I was a part of all that.

I jumped to my feet and screamed, "Pick out a good one, and send it out of here!" My teammates joined in. "Little bingle ... now's the time ... Little bingle ... get it going."

Whether Mills heard the chatter I don't know, but his energy seemed to grow, and his practice swings cut through the air with more power. Clayton looked in to Elliot for the sign. He took a big breath and dealt. The ball came to the plate in a big, sweeping curve that dipped low toward the outside of the plate. Mills took a big swing and hit the ball as solidly as any that day. The ball soared down the right field line and easily over the embankment out of reach of the right fielder.

"Foul ball," announced Ruggles in a matter-of-fact way, his voice sounding tired, lacking drama or conviction. The pronouncement was unneeded. Mills and everyone could see it was foul. I made a mental note that the sewer might give up another ball to me and my cousin Winston in a few days.

Roger started in for another conference at the mound, but Ruggles stepped two paces in front of the plate and waved him back. "Really, boys? Why don't we just play ball? Enough talking." Roger hit reverse without turning around, backpedaling to his position.

At this point all the enthusiasm was from our side. Our chatter drowned out our opponents. We could sense that Mills had the advantage and that some sort of hit seemed inevitable. But what happened next is one of those things in baseball that catches everyone by surprise. It was one of those things that can turn a game entirely around and give a team on the ropes the chance to storm back.

Mills hit the next pitch right on the fat part of the bat. It screamed directly back at Clayton so fast that he had no time to open his glove to grab it. The ball hit the outside of Clayton's glove and ricocheted high in the air and then fell directly to Roger. What should have been at least a leadoff single up the middle became out number one. That's baseball.

The out that should have been a hit changed the tone of the game. The other side became energized: their spirits lifted, and their chatter exploded. I sat on the bench between my teammates and thought how unfair that was. I heard someone say, "I'd rather be lucky than good."

As the other team whipped that ball around the infield in the standard ritual, Louie Page took his place in the batter's box. With his energy restored, Clayton came inside with a fastball and jammed Louie on the thin part of the bat. Louie took a defensive swing and weakly clanked the ball foul.

When a ball hits the bat close to where the batter holds it, the result is often painful. Louie dropped the bat and shook his hands. He spun around and walked away toward the bench, grimacing in pain. Dad checked his hands to make sure there was no real injury. Ruggles took a look too and, satisfied Louie could continue, motioned for him to return to play. When Louie did return to bat, he took a pitch for a called strike two and then waved ineffectually at strike three. He walked slowly back to the bench shaking his right hand, trying to get the feeling back in it.

Two outs. Bottom of the fifth inning. Score tied one each. But we had Billy coming to the plate. Although we had other good hitters, I remember thinking that if Billy did not do something and if we got too far down in the bottom of the lineup, we'd be in trouble. Billy, however, showed no emotion, certainly no desperation or pessimism. He walked to the plate looking much as I would going to the school lunchroom—not very excited about what was there but heading off to do something necessary.

Neither Billy nor Clayton seemed to have the energy or the interest in playing mind games. No stepping in and out of the batter's box, no shaking off signs, no calling teammates in for a conference on the mound. The first pitch came in hard and in the dirt for a ball. The second came right down the middle of the zone for strike one. Billy did not take the bat off of his shoulder for either one. He simply watched them come.

Clayton was working quickly, no waiting between pitches, just get the ball, get set, stand, and deliver. The third pitch was a slow curveball that dropped over the inside corner for strike two. Billy still had not made an effort to swing.

I was puzzled. I couldn't understand what was going on with Billy. Was he that tired? Did he just want to get it over and get home to dinner? He seemed resigned to being called out. Clayton got the ball back from Elliot and pounded it once, twice into his glove. He straightened his cap, looked down at Billy, and fired a fastball.

Billy responded with a quick, powerful swing. He contacted the ball cleanly and sent it high over the shortstop's head, rocketing ever higher between the left and center fielders. When the ball made it past Paul Fowler, it was clear it would be an extra base hit. As Billy crossed first base, he looked to see where the ball had traveled and whether or not Paul had chased it down. He saw what we all saw: only Paul's back as he ran full speed to catch up to the ball that was rolling far beyond him. Billy crossed second base and turned his eyes to third. He saw Dad, just on the home side of the base, waving his arms wildly, spinning like a windmill, urging him home. Billy's foot touched third base before Paul caught up to the ball, and there was no doubt he would score. Not even Paul had the arm to make that throw. By the time Billy crossed home plate with the go-ahead run, Elliot had already walked away to retrieve the catcher's mask that he had tossed aside in hopes of taking a throw for a play at the plate.

We swarmed Billy, a delirious, screaming group as he made his way back to the bench. Dad ran over to tell us to cut our celebrating, reminding us that there was still work to do—the game was not over. Several of their infielders gathered around the pitcher's mound, but no one spoke. Ruggles yelled to get the next batter up and play ball.

Druey Lambert hit the next pitch hard but directly to Herb Livertt at third. A good throw to first ended our half of the inning. As soon as the third out was official, Dad jumped to his feet pumping his fist. "Keep your heads up! Stay alive out there, and get this thing over with." We had the lead, two runs to one.

Those who play a lot of team sports will eventually have two kinds of experiences. In one case, nothing works out right. Losing can be not just humbling but humiliating. You may see the worst in an opponent who will not "play fair." And there can be times you see less than you would hope for in the behavior of those on your team.

But when you are at the other end—even if you don't win on the scoreboard—you have laudable adversaries, and you have people beside you that you hope to not let down. This was my first time on a real team, and it changed me in important ways. In future years I played a lot of sports. I paid for most of my college with sports scholarships. But even beyond those years I have always looked for teammates. I have had the good fortune to always find people with whom it was a privilege to share some kind of work beyond the playground. I have accomplished very little in life all by myself. Even now, I continue to seek out and to find others for my "team."

CHAPTER 15

Time and Timelessness

October 26th, 1945

Dear Charlotte,

Hello there honey, how are you? I have not got a letter from you since that one in which you had told me you had been sick, and I am getting worried about you. I am coming home to you and Chip though honey, I have got my orders and have taken all my things down to the plane terminal. Now all I have to do is sweat out a ride on a plane. They don't have planes coming through here like they used to and the ones that are coming through are already loaded with soldiers going home from bases south of here. They are supposed to have eight seats reserved for this base each day, but they never have that many and from three to six is all they get on a plane a day now. There are twenty men ahead of me on a waiting list so priorities and traffic told me it would probably be from three to five days before I get on a plane. I am coming home to you and Chip though for sure, and that makes me happy. So I don't mind sweating out a couple more days for a ride. I do hope that you are okay though honey. I hope I get a letter today saying that you are okay and everything is fine. I will be home in about eight or ten days, but I sure hope I get a letter from you before I leave here or I will be worried to death until I get home. Don't write to me anymore after you get this letter unless it is an emergency message and if there is an emergency message send it by wire, or through the Red Cross.

I am going to Ft. Bragg for discharge but I will have to stop at Miami Air Base, and Camp Blanding before going to Ft. Bragg. I don't know how long that will take, but I should be home not more than ten days after I leave this base. I am going to write more if I am going to be here a couple more days yet, and I am going to write one which I will not mail until right before getting on the plane, and I will write the date on the back of the envelope with pen or pencil and that will be the date I left here.

I'm all a flutter honey because I am coming home to my wife, and I am going to see that little old Chip of mine for the first time. Does he know that I am coming home honey?

Right now I am worried about you honey, and I sure hope that I get a letter today saying that you are okay, If you are not okay and have not sent me word by the time you get this letter try to get word to me at the separation center at Ft. Bragg.

If you are okay tell Chip that I am coming home and for him to move over.

Love,
Charlie

I DON'T KNOW IF all the waiting he did before being allowed to come home had anything to do with it, but my dad was fond of talking about time. He believed that baseball was unique in reference to the passing of time. He pointed out that baseball is the only game that has no time clock. It's the only game that could go on forever. There could be a game that never ended. Yes, golf and bowling have no time clock either, but no one plays defense in those games. A game with no defense is not much of a game, in his eyes. Plus, the structure of golf and bowling will bring the contest to an end eventually.

I reminded him more than once that tennis has no clock and that even a tiebreaker could go on forever if no one ever got ahead by two points, but he didn't really accept there was a real defense in tennis. Tennis players are on both offense and defense at the same time, doing the same thing—hitting the ball, trying to win a point—so no one really plays defense. He always believed he won the argument.

The possibility of a never-ending game aside, time was now running out for Paul and his team. Although still hours before sunset, some streaky, hazy clouds hid the sun but did little to lower the heat of the afternoon. The chalk lines for first and third base were still readable but smudged and erased at certain points. Eighteen sweaty, dust-covered boys prepared themselves for what was next. Our opponents faced their last at-bat, unless they could rally to tie the score. They seemed deflated; no chatter came from their bench.

For a moment the sluggish lack of energy colored our side as well. We took the field as if unsure how to act with the score in our favor. Dad brought this to an end as he barked, "Come on now! Let's see some hustle! Keep your heads up and your eyes open! Come on now!" We responded with a cacophony of chatter. Billy took the last of his warm-up throws, and we fired the ball around the infield.

"Hey, Babe, hey, Babe … you da one!"

"Come, Babe; hum, Babe ... Fire it in there ..."

"Batter up!" commanded Ruggles.

Herb Livertt, who had been left standing at home plate when Terry was thrown out to end the last inning, walked slowly to the batter's box. His vigorous practice cuts brought renewed energy to his team. They knew they had some of their best hitters coming to bat, including Paul Fowler up next. Clayton Lowman would follow. No need for giving up at this point.

I looked in at Billy from my position at second base. He had the same calm, almost-disinterested look on his face as when he hit the home run. He seemed to inhabit a world of his own. His first pitch hit the catcher's mitt with a sound like a gunshot.

"Streerriiike one!"

Herb watched the pitch fly by. His team again grew quiet. After a few more warm-up swings he watched the second pitch scream past him.

"Streerriiike two!"

Herb stepped out and stood looking hard at Billy. Billy patiently looked down at the ground and waited until Herb moved back in, and then he delivered the next pitch. Herb's swing was late, and the ball scorched Druey's mitt for strike three before Herb completed his swing. Ruggles didn't bother to call the strike out loud but simply raised his right hand in silent affirmation of out number one.

Now it was Paul Fowler's turn. Paul matched Billy's focus in what needed to be done. No scowling, no mind games: just go through the rituals, and do what needed to be done. Tap the plate. Hitch the pants. Touch the cap. Bend at the knees. Spit. Cock the bat, and be ready. This was the showdown. This is what it should have all come down to.

Billy delivered the first pitch, changing his approach, knowing his opponent. He let up on a slow, sweeping curveball that caught Paul swinging too early. Paul tipped the ball with the very end of his bat, and it squibbed away harmlessly into foul territory.

Paul stepped away, and I think I saw a look of uncertainty or doubt creep into his expression. At times baseball is a guessing game. There are only a few types of pitches that any pitcher can throw. It's mostly about speed and location of the ball when it reaches the plate. Fast or slow, curve or changeup, inside of the strike zone to crowd the batter or sweeping away on the outside corner, high and tight or low and away. One element of success is to throw the unexpected pitch. If the batter guesses right and is waiting for the pitch that comes, then good things happen for the batter. But at this point Paul looked as if he had no idea what Billy was going to throw him next.

The next pitch came in much like the first—a curveball, not very fast. But Paul had guessed fastball. He tried hard to adjust as he saw the ball coming in slow and fat, a pitch he ought to hit, but his timing was off again, and his swing missed awkwardly.

Paul called time-out and asked Ruggles for a moment to change to a different bat. Request granted, Paul took his position with a smaller, lighter bat, for better control. Maybe he was stalling for time. He did not have Billy figured out, and he needed to think. Would Billy throw a third curveball? Not likely. Would he try to surprise Paul with his fastest pitch, now that Paul had looked at two slow ones? Would the change in the weight of the bat make Billy change his approach? Take a guess.

Paul readied himself. Tap. Hitch. Touch the cap. Bend. Spit. Cock the bat. Find a way to hit the ball. No infield chatter now. Everyone there, on the field or just watching, held their breath. I prayed. *Please don't make me have to handle another Paul Fowler bullet.*

Billy threw the fastball. Paul responded quickly with a mighty cut but hit just under the ball and lifted a towering fly ball to centerfield. The ball hung in the sky forever, a small white speck against faded blue. Louie settled under it; the long wait found him shuffling his feet for balance, awkward, uncertain. Ultimately the ball fell safely into his glove. We all exhaled, knowing that Paul had just barely missed. If he had swung a half inch higher, he would have hit the ball so far that he could have crawled around the bases. Maybe if he had kept the heavier bat.

Two outs and their pitcher Clayton stepped up to the plate as the last chance for them to get something going. Perhaps a game like this should have ended more dramatically, but I think after Paul's out all the spirit had left the opposition. I'm not saying Clayton himself quit, but his soft ground ball down the first baseline on the first pitch rolled directly to Jerry. Jerry fielded it cleanly, stepped on the bag, and the game was over.

We jumped around and hugged each other for the longest time. Dad stood back. He had a big smile on his face yet was measurably restrained, as if to say, "Don't get too excited about this." He motioned for us to join him in shaking hands with the other team, but by the time we made our way over to the other side, most of them had already picked up their gear and were up the bank for the walk or ride home.

∞

I know this was just one game in a very small community. I recently talked by phone with Billy Cline, and he "sort of" remembered the game, his incomplete memory understandable given his remarkable athletic journey through college and professional sports. I wonder who of the other players remembers the game. Some of the boys on the field that day went home to difficult family situations, so what importance would such a game have for them?

The game was much more important to me. I took inspiration from my induction into the membership of sports teams. While I paid for most of my college with basketball scholarships, my heart will always belong to baseball.

∞

In 1974 the Hildebran school system consolidated with other smaller schools in the area and ceased to exist as a high school. In 1987 the community conducted a homecoming, celebrating all the graduates of Hildebran. All class years were invited. We celebrated with alumni basketball games for boys and for girls and a parade through the town that still looked much as it did in 1957.

In the evening, the school's collection of sports trophies were auctioned and proceeds given to benefit a local library. The only trophy not up for auction was the one for the 1964 state basketball championship.

This was removed from the auction block and presented to the coach of that team, Melvin Ruggles.

My dad and I looked over the various trophies before the auction, and he noticed a tall, silver-plated loving cup that bore the inscription "Burke County Field Day" with the initial date of 1926. It survived from a time when the small schools of the area had insufficient funds and population to support teams in their modern form. The cup was awarded each year to the school that won an annual field day, engraved each time with the school name and the date. The final engraving was 1940.

"I remember this cup … I helped Valdese win it one year!" He spoke with more spark and enthusiasm than had become customary for him in his seventieth year. He told the story of winning the shot put that day, putting Valdese in the victory circle. He ran his finger over the engraving for "Valdese High School 1937." Not feeling well, he went home before the auction itself. I promised him I would buy it for him. The auction turned out to be one last competition that he and I would share.

For the auction everyone gathered in the old school cafeteria, the one in which I cowered in shyness from the incidental gaze of pretty girls and where I was teased by bigger students. I was never really bullied, thanks to my older brother. The rules of the auction specified that if someone present had a clear connection to a trophy, he or she would be allowed to buy it for just a few dollars. Most went for ten to fifteen. I split a few with my buddy Dale Abernathy. But one trophy that did not fall in that category turned out to be the loving cup. A graduate named Francis Orders, an antique dealer, saw profit in buying and reselling the cup.

Francis clearly had a figure in mind that he was willing to pay. When he and I bid it up to $120, the room started to buzz. I didn't really know what it was worth in the marketplace and what he would be willing to spend, and he did not know that I would pay whatever it took.

At $200 the room stopped buzzing and erupted with cheering, chattering, and trash-talking. They urged us up and on. I had classmates there, and so did he. I'm not sure how others chose sides, but the room seemed about equally split and loud for each of us.

"It's yours, Francis! Don't be a pussy; buy the damn thing!" a voice rang out over the crowd.

"Come on, Drew … You can't let him get away with that!" someone else offered.

With the bidding at $240, Francis walked back up to the front and took one last look to see if he could justify continuing the bid. In the end I wrote a check for the library and took the trophy home to Dad. My sister told me later that he had paced around the house repeating, "I sure hope Drew buys that trophy for me."

Before going home I walked down to the baseball field with my four-year-old daughter. It was still early and with just enough daylight left to run around the bases with her and look over the embankment at the sewer that claimed all the baseballs. After that I didn't go back to the field for ten years. Then in July 1997, my dad died, and I had to go there again, to my field of dreams and my place to run to. I sat in the outfield grass and cried.

CHAPTER 16

Soldier Comes Home

Hey there wifey, I have got my orders and I am coming home to you and Chip finally. This is the letter which I said I would write and mail just before getting on the plane. I will write the date on the back of the envelope in pen or pencil in figures and that will be the date I have left here.

I am glad I am coming home to you and that little old Chip, and I should be there in ten days after the date you will see on the back of the envelope.

Bye for now, and it won't be long until I will be right there with you and Chip to stay with you all the time.

Love,
Charlie

ON THE BACK OF this letter he wrote the number twenty-eight. A close examination of the number shows that he first wrote twenty-seven and then marked over the seven with an eight. I'm not sure if he at first wrote the wrong number, uncertain of the date, or whether he started to board and was told he had to wait one more day. It doesn't matter now. He made it home. Yet those small details intrigue me, especially since he is gone.

I think there are such things as key moments early in life. One baseball game in a ten-year-old boy's life may seem small and inconsequential, but I think that day, that game, changed me. Perhaps the more important part of the day came as my brother, father, and I returned home. Just before Dad turned his attention back to farm chores, he took me aside, looked down at the scorebook in his hand, slapped the page for emphasis, and said, "You know, if you had not caught that ball in the first inning, we would not have won that game." He pulled his baseball cap tighter on his head and walked away toward the barn.

I wandered away, or perhaps it would be better to say I *floated* away, filled with pride that I had been a part of that game and, more importantly, that I'd won the praise of my father. I walked down the hill to the left of our garden—beyond the flowering crepe myrtles, past the grapevines, the apple trees, and the wisteria draped over the large oak there—and leaned my back against the largest trunk of a chinaberry tree. At that moment the world was filled with infinite possibility. No prince ever stood in a more fabulous kingdom.

As I have written throughout, this is not the story of my father as a perfect man. But together with my mother and key people in my community, he did what parents need to do sufficiently well so that I could grow up, leave home, and not need them anymore.

I have lived a remarkable life, although remarkable mostly to me.

I attended college, succeeded in sports well enough to ultimately be named to a small-college sports hall of fame. I attended medical school and have practiced psychiatry for thirty-six years and counting, as of 2014. I have a daughter who is smarter, stronger, and more courageous than I have ever been. I endured the death of my wife of twenty-nine years, the lovely and loving mother of my daughter, and I am now remarried to the most creative, smart, strong, and beautiful woman on the planet.

Of course I owe most of this good life to those I took as first models. Many teachers and coaches come to mind, but my father was the first. As late in life as when I was fifty years old, when my father had grown frail and thin and somewhat out of touch with how the world had turned, I still saw him as a refuge. I told myself that if I was ever in any real trouble or needed a protector, I would go find him. His passing does not fully diminish his value as my defender. He is still there in what I have learned, how I have developed, and who I am.

AFTERWORD

HOW MUCH OF THIS story is true? With the scorebook for this game lost, I certainly do not remember all the boys who played in the game. There is no way I could have accurately recreated the detail represented in the play-by-play. Clayton, Roger, Paul, and Terry were there, and Billy, Druey, my brother, and I played. I think I have some of the others right, but I chose to include some of them simply because they were some of the most interesting boys in my childhood. I think I have recreated the true spirit of that game.

I included the action involving Paul hitting the ball off the house and Mickey making the phantom catch down the embankment because both were oft-repeated legends of that playing field. Did those legends actually begin with incidents in that particular game? The reader should take joy in the question. I do remember Billy winning the game with a home run. The score ended two to one. And I did get an unassisted double play in the first inning; my dad talked about it for years.

Nothing would please me more than for a couple dozen or so boys, now men, to come forward and say they actually played in that game and I wrongly left them out. In fact, hundreds of boys in the following years played baseball in local sports programs because of the efforts of my dad, Ruggles, Ray Childers, Clyde Houston, and the other men who put in the time to establish Little League baseball in Hildebran. We had formal teams with real uniforms by the time I was twelve years old.

The narrative of my childhood experiences with my cousin Winston and the telling of the other family stories is how I truly remember it all. How much can one trust the accuracy of memories from fifty-eight years ago? I purposely distorted nothing.

My father's letters are not edited. I have taken great pains to simply retype them as he put the words on the page.

Even though we stayed in Hildebran, I never made it to first base with Geraldine.

If I have offended anyone with how I have told this story, I apologize. Consider how clueless I was in those days and maybe still am.

My grandmother, Laura Ida Miller Yoder

The old homeplace in Hildebran, North Carolina (1957)

Charlotte and Charlie Bridges, my parents

Me, age twelve

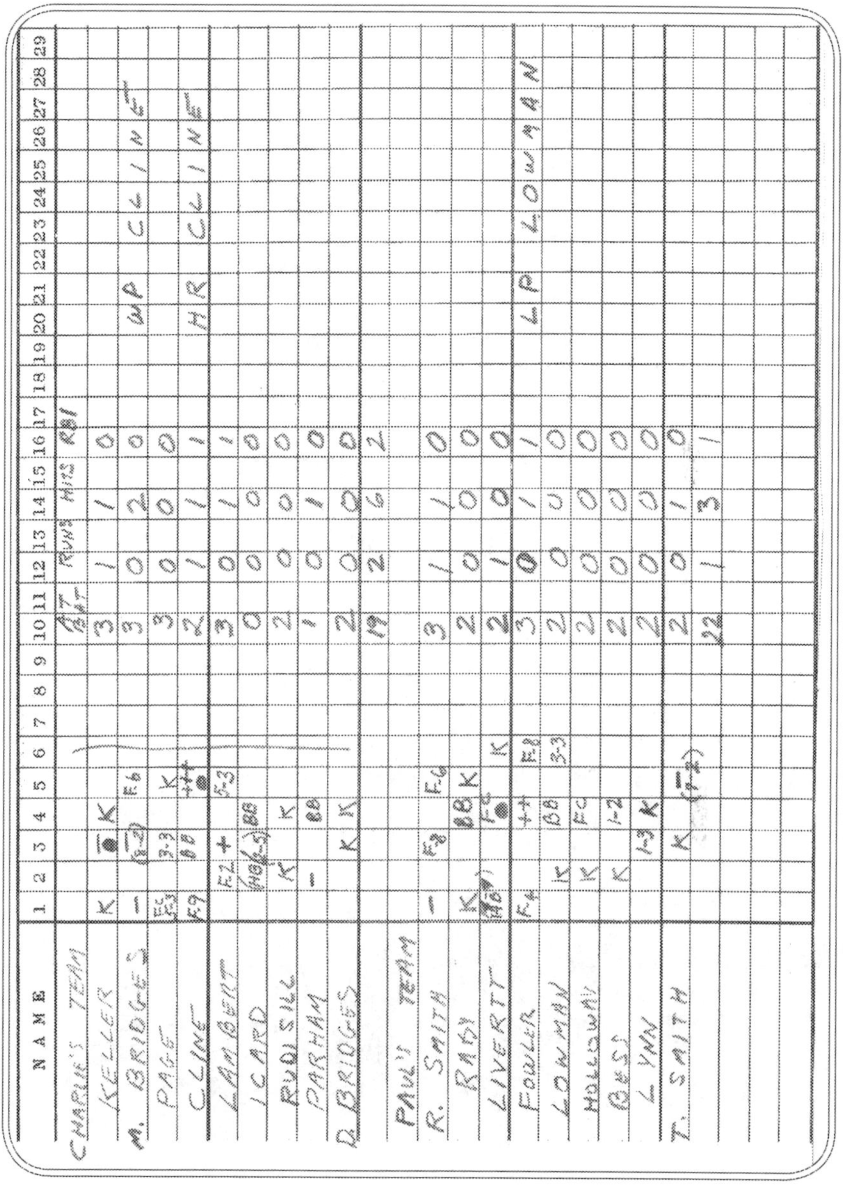

NAME	1	2	3	4	5	6	AT BAT	RUNS	HITS	RBI	
CHARLIE'S TEAM											
KELLER	K		●	K			3	1	1	0	
M. BRIDGES	–		(5-2)		F6		3	0	2	0	WP CLINE
PAGE	FC 5-3		3-3		K		3	0	0	0	
CLINE	F9		BB		+++ ●		2	1	1	1	HR CLINE
LAMBERT		F2	+		5-3		3	0	1	1	
ICARD		(HB)	(5-5)	BB			0	0	0	0	
RUDISILL		K		K			2	0	0	0	
PARHAM		–		BB			1	0	1	0	
D. BRIDGES			K	K			2	0	0	0	
							19	2	6	2	
PAUL'S TEAM											
R. SMITH	–		F8		F6		3	1	1	0	
RABY	K			BB	K		2	0	0	0	
LIVERITT	HB			FC ●		K	2	1	0	0	
FOWLER	F4			++		F8	3	0	1	1	LP LOWMAN
LOWMAN		K		BB		3-3	2	0	0	0	
HOLLOWAY		K		FC			2	0	0	0	
BESS		K		1-2			2	0	0	0	
LYNN			1-3	K			2	0	0	0	
T. SMITH			K		(F2)		2	0	1	0	
							22	1	3	1	

Recreated box score of the second-greatest game

Burke County Field Day trophy

The Hildebran baseball field

Charlie's letters

Ford woody toy reproduction

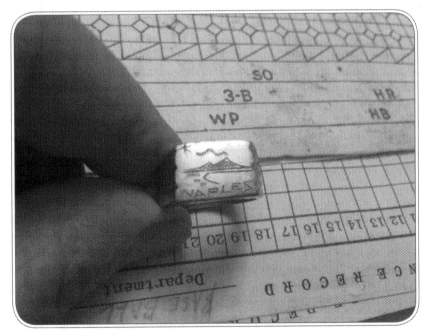

Ring made in Italy by roadside blacksmith artist

A FINAL NOTE

A Testimonial

IN 2009 THE HILDEBRAN High School class of 1964 held its forty-fifth reunion. Attendees were asked to speak about someone who had a positive influence on them in their growing-up years. Gary Wilkerson, a year older than me, and the point guard on Melvin Ruggles's state champion basketball team, chose to remember my father. He described Dad's efforts to organize local boys for involvement in the local basketball program. What follows is taken from his talk.

∽

Hauling kids in the woody actually began with baseball, not basketball. He, Ray Childers, Melvin Ruggles, and a few others were essentially the founders of Little League baseball in Hildebran. Until it started in an organized way, Mr. Bridges carried carloads of boys to Hickory.

Basketball soon followed. Some of the boys that went to Valdese for the league there were Tommy Keller, Louie Page, Bobby and Willis Burkette, and Jerry Rudisill. I really don't know how I got invited to ride in the old woody wagon to Valdese. However, I'm fairly sure that Coach Ruggles had something to do with it. At that time I was twelve years old with no basketball or goal in the backyard. I couldn't dribble or shoot. However, Coach Ruggles had introduced me to a jump rope and explained to me that I needed to engage in something only girls do. But that is another story.

Anyway, I crawled into that woody on my ride to Valdese for the first time. All the talk was about a young man from Valdese who was "all that." His name was Joe Brown, and according to all the other boys he was just the greatest. I remember walking into the Valdese YMCA on that Friday night as if it were yesterday. There was this tall, young athlete dribbling the ball between his legs and gliding to the basket effortlessly. He was dunking on the eight-foot goals with ease. I couldn't even touch the rim. The jump rope had not taken effect yet.

There I was watching the greatest basketball player ever. I studied his movements closely and concluded that the dark, olive-skin boy was indeed talented, but when I measured him and weighed him, *I found him lacking!*

First he was a year younger than me. Age counts for something. He lived in town. I lived in the country. I cut pulpwood and ran a chain saw. Therefore I concluded that I had to be stronger than him. I decided that he wasn't nearly as fast as me or as quick. The rest of the story is that when I was a senior in high school and his Valdese team came to our gym, I remember drawing three charges on him halfway through the second quarter.

The second most defining moment of my young basketball career occurred when Mr. Bridges took us to Cool Springs, North Carolina. When we exited that old woody, we were ready to put a whooping on those boys from Cool Springs.

When we entered the gym, there must have been some kind of mistake, because I'm positive that one or two of their players had driven there. They were big and ugly. Mr. Bridges was talking to the other coach, and after a few minutes we decided that we would play them anyway, since we had driven that far.

I thought, *Well, I'm not a starter. I only get to play about a minute at the end of the first and second half—so how bad can it be.* I took my position at the end of the bench when Mr. Bridges looked at me and said, "Gary, I want you to start today." I thought to myself, *Oh, please no, no!* Anyway, Mr. Bridges assigned me to guard the strongest and biggest boy on their team. He was a foot taller and at least three years older.

I got near this guy and could smell the rubbing alcohol he had splashed on his face after shaving that morning. To say the least, I was terrified. Soon Mr. Bridges called time-out. He asked me if everything was okay. I said yes but asked if he didn't think that Mills should play that boy. He said, "I want you to play him. And have you really looked at him?" I thought, *Are you crazy? Of course I've looked at him.*

Mr. Bridges said, "You know, that boy is bigger than you, but I believe you are about as strong as him." Well, how did Mr. Bridges know that? Of course I was as strong; in fact, I was a whole lot quicker and faster. When I went back out on the court, I beat him half to death. Every time he took a step, I was already standing where he wanted to be. I even gave him a couple of kidney punches when the refs weren't looking so he would know I was there.

When the game was over, Mr. Bridges did not say "Good game." He didn't really say anything, but I could tell he was proud of me. Further, I walked with him to the old woody with his arm around me. The boy I had beaten up in the gym was waiting for me in the parking lot, but I wasn't quite ready to deal with that.

So there you have it. No matter whether I played with you or against you, you were measured and weighed *and found lacking* because I was stronger, faster, quicker, and, if necessary, meaner than you.

I reflect on the example Mr. Bridges was setting for a young man like me: his commitment to his sons and others to take us to Valdese for a game on Friday night, working at the bakery the rest of the night, and getting us back to Valdese for practice on Saturday.

Charles Steven Bridges is someone I hold in high esteem! He was setting a lifelong example for all of us on how to live our life. Someone I have the utmost respect for, and I appreciate him for believing in me before I believed in myself.

—GARY WILKERSON, *Hildebran High School class of '64*

⌦

Author's note: The boy named Joe Brown in Gary Wilkerson's comments played basketball for the UNC Tarheels in the late 1960s. UNC basketball coach Dean Smith did not find him lacking. Gary must have made him stronger.